THE MOGUL EMPERORS OF HINDUSTAN

THE MOGUL EMPERORS OF HINDUSTAN

A. D. 1398 - A.D. 1707

EDWARD S. HOLDEN

OFTEN AN ACTION OF SMALL NOTE, A SHORT SAYING OR A JEST, SHALL DISTINGUISH A PERSON'S REAL CHARACTER MORE THAN THE GREATEST SIEGES-PLUTARCH

GYAN

Published by

Gyan Publishing House
5, Ansari Road
Daryaganj, New Delhi-110002
Phone: 011-47034999, 9811692060
E-mail: books@gyanbooks.com

Distribution Network
gyanbooks.com
India, USA, Canada, UK, Australia, France

ISBN : 978-81-212-3785-7 (PB)
First Published, London, 1895

2nd Impression 2020

Printed at: Gyan Press, Delhi.

The Mogul Emperors of Hindustan
Author: Edward S. Holden

THE MOGUL EMPERORS OF HINDUSTAN

A.D. 1398–A.D. 1707

BY

EDWARD S. HOLDEN, LL.D.

Often an action of small note, a short saying or a jest, shall distinguish a person's real character more than the greatest sieges.—PLUTARCH.

Westminster

ARCHIBALD CONSTABLE AND CO.

PUBLISHERS TO THE INDIA OFFICE

14 PARLIAMENT STREET

1895

The Empress Mumtaz-I-Mahal

Buried in the Taj Mahal 1631

INTRODUCTORY NOTE

A COLLECTION of miniatures of the Mogul emperors, some of which are copied in this book, came into my hands many months ago. The accounts of these unfamiliar personages which are given in the ordinary books of reference I found to be inadequate and frequently incorrect. Accordingly, I devoted the spare hours of a long and harassing winter to reading the original memoirs of the native historians of India and the accounts of early ambassadors and travellers to the court of the Great Moguls. A few of these I wrote out in brief, and they were printed in various periodicals. I have been asked to reprint them in a more complete form, which I am very glad to do, as I know of no one volume which contains the information here collected.

To those who have lived or travelled in India, the subject of this book will be more or less familiar, since the jurisprudence, customs, and architecture of the Mogul emperors have left remains which still serve to recall their authors. Yet I think that even this class of readers may find it convenient to have many scattered fragments of biography and history brought together in one place. To the majority of persons, however, the Mogul period is a closed one; it is hardly more than a name; its impulses are alien, its note is foreign, and its history seems remote. But even to us, who are so far removed in time and in temper, it is not without interest to study the characters of the kings who ruled India for three eventful centuries; and it is chiefly to the latter class of readers that this book is addressed.

I wish to emphasize the fact that its chapters are not intended to give the *history* of the reigns in question, but rather to present such views of the chief personages involved as an intelligent reader of the histories themselves might wish to carry away. The materials which I have used are to be found in all great libraries, although they are dispersed in very many different volumes. Moreover, the writings of Oriental biographers require to be worked over into a new shape before they are acceptable to Western readers.

I have not encumbered these pages with the host of foot-notes which would be necessary had I referred by work, volume, and page to their sources. It may suffice to say that the chief authorities consulted have been the Memoirs of the emperors themselves; the standard histories of Persia, India, and Tartary, by Elphinstone, Malcolm, Erskine, Price, Hunter, Howorth, and others; the records of early missions and voyages; and, more especially, the invaluable translations of the native historians, by Sir Henry Elliot, Professor Dowson, and Professor Blochmann; in short, all the works that I was able to find which treat of the subject in hand.

The very interesting lives of Akbar, by Colonel Malleson and Comte F. A. de Noer, and of Aurangzeb, by Mr. Stanley Lane-Poole, came into my hands after this book was finished. I have carefully compared Chapters IV and VII with these, the latest authorities, but I have seen nothing to change. As a matter of fact, all histories of the Moguls must depend upon the same originals. The interpretation of these originals rests with the reader. I have attempted to present them so fully as to make the interpretation easy. Whenever it was possible, I have used the very words of the various chronicles; and this must be my excuse for some inconsistencies in spelling, etc. I have also chosen to retain the spelling of the word *Mogul*, which a usage of more than two centuries has made familiar to English readers, rather than to introduce the more correct form, *Mughal*.

I count myself particularly fortunate in that I have the permission of Sir William Hunter to reprint (in Chapter VIII) his masterly picture of the downfall of the last of the great Mogul emperors.

I have been able to find nearly all the original authorities for this book in the libraries of the Pacific Coast, which seems to be not a little remarkable when it is considered how far removed our American interests, literary and otherwise, are from those of India, especially of mediæval India. Other works I have consulted by the courtesy of Dr. Justin Winsor, Librarian of Harvard University.

There was every reason to expect that no complete series of entirely authentic portraits of the Mogul emperors could be obtained. So far as I have been able to discover, there is no such series in America. By the liberal action of the authorities of the British Museum, and through the very kind offices of Dr. Richard Garnett, keeper of its printed books, and of Professor Robert K. Douglas, keeper of Oriental Mss., I received permission to copy the portraits of the Mogul kings from a collection of rare and exquisite Indian drawings by contemporary artists, which constitutes one of its many treasures. The group of four emperors—Babar, Humayun, Akbar, Jahangir—which is given at the beginning of Chapter II, is reproduced from a Ms. of the *Shah-Jahan-Nameh* (British Museum

Add., 20,734), which was formerly in the possession of Akbar III, King of Delhi. The portrait of Shah Jahan as an old man (page 270), and of Aurangzeb (page 309), are from Ms. Add., 18,801.

These plates were kindly selected for me by Mr. H. Arthur Doubleday of London, publisher to the India Office, who also was good enough to superintend their photographic reproduction from the original Mss. The portraits are entirely authentic; with one exception they have never before been printed; indeed, their existence was only known to a few Oriental scholars; and they have the additional advantage of exhibiting Indian portraiture at its best, in everything but color.

The frontispiece of this book, from an exquisite miniature on ivory, is a copy of a picture given to my son by Sir Edwin Arnold. The plate of Akbar, Nur-Mahal, and Shah Jahan (as a young man) is reproduced from other miniatures in my collection. They purport to be copies of original portraits. How faithfully, even slavishly, such originals are copied and recopied I have learned by comparing two photographs of Nur-Mahal in my possession. One of these is after a miniature now in London, the other after a miniature now in Delhi. The two miniatures were copied from the same original. The closest scrutiny fails to detect any difference whatever in any part of the two photographs. The very pattern of a rug is absolutely identical in the two copies of copies. Hence it is that one comes to have confidence in such reproductions by Indian artists. The spirited design of two Asiatic warriors used as a stamp on the cover, is after a Persian painting of the time of Marco Polo, *circa* A.D. 1300, and it is reproduced from Colonel Yule's remarkable life of the great traveller.

The portrait of Nur-Mahal (Nur-Jahan) at the beginning of Chapter VI, is copied from an engraving which bears the title "Noor Jehan, or the Light of the World, after an original drawing from the library of the Great Mogul, and now in the possession of the Publishers," which is further marked "P. 185." I do not know to what work this belongs, but this rare portrait is evidently a faithful copy of some Indian original, and is extremely interesting.

The view of the tomb of Tamerlane, in Samarkand, is redrawn from a photograph which I owe to the kindness of Professor D. Gedeonof, Director of the Observatory of Tashkend. From Rousselet's *India and its Native Princes* the following cuts are taken (by permission of the publishers): The Tomb of Humayun, the Mosque of Aurangzeb at Benares. The view of the Taj-Mahal is made from a negative by Mr. Frederick Diodati Thompson of New York, and first appeared in his book, *In the Track of the Sun.* It is printed by permission of Messrs. D. Appleton & Co. These characteristic views of famous buildings illustrate the progress (and decay) of Mogul architecture from the time of Tamerlane (1400) to the reign of Aurangzeb (1700). Finally, the drawing of the lotus (page 365) is reduced from a native Indian picture, in colors, in the collection of Miss Olive Risley-Seward of Washington.

Professor Gedeonof, Director of the Imperial Observatory of Tashkend, Professor C. Michie Smith, Director of the Observatory of Madras, Mr. Thomas G. Allen of New Jersey, and, especially, Mr. H. Arthur Doubleday of London, have been most kind in procuring for me miniatures and photographic copies of portraits and views. I have to express my grateful thanks to Miss Agnes Clerke for researches made in the collections of the British Museum, and to Miss Sara Carr Upton for similar researches made in the Library of Congress and elsewhere.

Through the thoughtful kindness of many friends in many parts of the world it has thus been possible to collect in this one volume illustrations of the personages and of the architecture of the India of long ago. I beg to express my sincere obligations to them all; and also to my publishers for the pains they have taken to present the illustrations in a fitting and artistic manner.

A mere chance originally drew my attention to the subject of this book; the leisure hours of a long winter were given to the study of the writings and characters of great rulers and great men like Babar and Akbar. If I have succeeded in conveying the impressions which I received, I shall be more than gratified.

E. S. H.

THE LICK OBSERVATORY,
MOUNT HAMILTON, April, 1893.

TABLE OF CONTENTS

PAGE

CHAPTER VI.

CHAPTER VII.

CHAPTER VIII.

CHAPTER IX.

LIST OF ILLUSTRATIONS

THE MOGUL EMPERORS OF HINDUSTAN

CHAPTER I

TAMERLANE THE GREAT

(BORN A.D. 1336, DIED 1405)

THE inhabitants of a small Italian city became the rulers of the world from the Euphrates to the cliffs of Albion. We are the inheritors of their civilization, and their history is taught to our little children. Their language and literature are as familiar as our own. The lives of their rulers and great men are part of the common stock of knowledge. We understand their characters, their aspirations, their most secret motives.

Centuries after Rome was famous the

hordes of Tartar and Mongol tribes in the far East gathered strength under great commanders. and overran what they also called "the inhabitable world," from Poland to the Persian Gulf and Hindustan ; from Constantinople to the China Sea ; from Corea to the Ganges. Their descendants founded a stable empire in India, which lasted until our own day. What living idea can we form of such alien personalities as those of Chengiz-Khan, of Tamerlane,. or of their great successors, Babar and Akbar? Shakspeare's play of *Julius Cæsar* might serve as a first text-book of Roman history in our schools to-day. Marlowe's scarcely less famous *Tamburlaine* is ludicrously inadequate as a picture of the Grand Khan of Tartary.

These people have never yet touched our national or our racial life. They are utter foreigners. We can understand the Moors in Spain ; and the chivalric Saladin is hardly stranger to us than Richard the Lion-Heart, or Saint Louis of France. But our interest in the Mongols is a mere intellectual inquisitiveness. If one seeks to satisfy this curiosity, one meets with singular difficulties. Not only are the character and motives of particular individuals quite alien to our own, but their very histories are given in foreign forms which perplex and confuse. It is perfectly simple to understand that Ulugh Beg, the grandson of Tamerlane, built in 1437, at Samarkand, the greatest astronomical observatory of the world, one hundred and forty years before Tycho Brahe erected Uranibourg in Denmark. But it is almost impossible to comprehend the intrigues and violence which deposed this good prince, and led to his death at the hands of his own son. As in this case, so in others. A consecutive history, by a native writer, of the reigns of Chengiz or of Timur (Tamerlane, "the lame prince"), seems totally unconnected and illogical. Its sanguinary pages record a hell which seems to be purposeless—without an object.

If we wish to satisfy the curiosity to know something, at least, of the character and motives of a sovereign like Timur, the simplest process is to collect the narratives of men of our own world who were eye-witnesses of his actions. These recitals give us the perspective outlines, which are intelligible even if they are not complete. The details of the sketch must be filled up by extracts from the native writers, and we have to choose such as seem *to us* significant. Finally, it may be possible, though difficult, to fit this picture into its place in the view of the world which we have inherited from our Roman ancestors and adopted for ourselves; and it is of the first importance to recollect that Rome was nearly two thousand years old when Mongol history begins.

An Embassy to the Grand Khan of Tartary

(A.D. 1254)

In the year 1248 Saint Louis of France embarked for the Holy Land. While he was yet at Cyprus he received ambassadors from the Grand Khan of Tartary, and understood, quite erroneously, that the Khan had been converted to Christianity. It seems to be true that he desired to attack the Saracens from one side, while the Crusaders advanced from the other. From Syria the King sent one William de Rubruquis, a monk of the order of the Friars Minors, as a sort of ambassador to Tartary. His real mission was to spy out the land, and to make such converts as he could. De Rubruquis was "a person of admirable parts, great diligence, unaffected piety and probity." His letter to the King, giving an account of his extraordinary journey, fully bears out this praise and deserves to be read in full. De Rubruquis left Constantinople for Tartary in May, 1253, and arrived at the court of Batu, the grandson of Chengiz-Khan (born 1162, died 1227), after months of perilous travel.

The subjects of Tamerlane were very like those of Chengiz-Khan. The acceptance of Islam was the only marked change, and the new religion was held but lightly. There is no better way to obtain a view of them than to copy a few paragraphs from the journal of the good monk:

"And after we departed out of those precincts we found the Tartars, amongst whom being entered, methought I was come into a new world, whose life and manners I will describe unto your Highness as well as I can. They have no settled habitation; neither know they to-day where they shall lodge to-morrow. They have all Scythia to themselves, which stretcheth from the river Danube to the utmost extent of the East. Each of their Captains, according to the number of his people, knows the bounds of his pastures, and where he ought to feed his cattle, winter and summer, spring and autumn. Their houses they raise upon a round foundation of wickers, artificially wrought and compacted together; the roof, consisting of wickers also, meeting above in one little roundell, which they cover with white (or black) felt. This cupola they adorn with variety of pictures."

The houses were moved from place to place on immense wagons twenty feet wide, drawn by two-and-twenty oxen in two rows, eleven in a row. "The axle-tree of the cart was of a huge bigness, like the mast of a ship. Batu (grandson of Chengiz-Khan) hath sixteen wives, every one of whom hath a great house. Hence it is that the court of a rich Tartar will appear like a very large village."

At the camps the houses were dismounted from the carts and ranged in order. The beds and furniture had particular and unvarying situations within the house. "There is a little lean idol which is, as it were, the guardian of the whole house. One piece of ceremony is constant in all houses; namely, a bench, on which stands a vessel of milk and cups for drinking it. In the summer-time they care not for any drink but *cosmos.**

"In respect to their food, give me leave to inform your Highness that, without difference or distinction, they eat all their beasts that die of age or sickness."

The customs and the laws of the Tartars are described at great length. The chief punishments are flogging and death.

"On my arrival among these barbarous

* Mares' milk—*koumiss.*

people I thought, as I before observed, that I was come into a new world. The first question they asked was whether we had ever been with them heretofore or not; and made us wait a long while, begging our bread from us, wondering at all things they saw, and desiring to have them. It is true they took nothing by force from me, but they will beg all they see, very importunately; and if a man bestows anything upon them it is but lost, for they are thankless wretches. So we departed from them; and indeed it seemed to me that we escaped out of the hands of devils."

On his journey he was presented to Zagatai, another grandson of Chengiz-Khan, and entered into his presence "with fear and bashfulness." The reception was not unfavorable, though the monk's gifts were few.

"I expounded to him the Apostles' Creed, which, after he had heard, he shook his head." The interpreter, however, was "a sorry one."

They still "went towards the eastward, seeing naught but the sky and the earth," till they reached their journey's end. At the court of the Khan they found a kind of comfort; even luxury of a sort. What is most surprising, they met with Nestorian and Jacobite priests in numbers; with fugitive Russians, Greeks, Hungarians, Muhammadans, in plenty; a Knight Templar, a French goldsmith, William Bouchier of Paris, and his wife, "a woman from Metz in Lorraine," and even with a strayed Englishman. This was more than a hundred years before the time of Timur, and it affords an explanation of the variety of arts known in Samarkand in his reign. The Tartar and Mongol tribesmen were still the same in his time, except for a nominal conformity to Islam. Christianity had been brought to Khorassan in the fourth century by the Nestorians. There was a Nestorian bishop in Merv in A.D. 334, and in Herat and Samarkand in A.D. 500. The Kerait Turkomans accepted Christianity about A.D. 1000, as a tribe. Buddhism came through China into Transoxania; and Islam crossed the Persian frontiers not long after the death of the Prophet. All these creeds were tolerated by Chengiz Khan.

The tolerance of Chengiz and his sons had ceased under Timur, and the Muslim *mollahs* ruled in all religious matters. But the arts of the architect, the goldsmith, the armorer, the weaver, had already been transplanted to these wilds from Europe, from China, from Africa, from Arabia, from Persia. Astronomy, mathematics, poetry, learning of a sort were cultivated, and the field was prepared for that remarkable advance in some of the arts (notably in architecture), which marks the period of Timur and his immediate successors.*

An Embassy to Tamerlane the Great (A.D. 1403)

King Henry III. of Castile (A.D. 1376–1407) despatched embassies to many princes of Europe and Asia. Tamerlane sent in return an envoy, Muhammad-al-Cazi, with presents and a letter. When the Mogul envoy

* For a very interesting description of the fine monuments of Samarkand in Timur's lifetime, see an article by M. Edouard Blanc in the *Revue des Deux Mondes* for February 15, 1893.

THE TOMB OF TIMUR

was to return, the King of Castile sent with him an embassy to the court of Timur Beg. Ruy Gonzales de Clavijo, one of the envoys, has left us an account of his perilous mission, which set out from Seville in May, 1403, and arrived at Samarkand in August, 1404, after traversing the Mediterranean and Euxine seas to Trebizond, and passing by land through Erzeroum, Teheran, near Merv, and across the Oxus to Samarkand—over seventy degrees of longitude.

In October, 1403, the ambassadors were received in audience by Manuel, the Emperor of Constantinople; and as they much desired to have a sight of the various Christian relics for which the churches of the city * were famous, special privileges were granted to them. The son-in-law of the Emperor acted as their guide in their pious visits. The Emperor himself was the custodian of the keys to the reliquaries. In the church of St. John the Baptist they saw the "left arm of St. John. This arm was withered so that the skin and bone alone remained, and the

* There were three thousand churches.

joints of the elbow and the hand were adorned with jewels." In another church they saw the saint's right arm, "and this was fresh and healthy." "And though they say that the whole body of the blessed St. John was destroyed except one finger, with which he pointed when he said, '*Ecce Agnus Dei!*' yet certainly the whole of this arm was in good preservation."* In various shrines they saw pieces of the true cross, made from the cross which the blessed St. Helena brought (entire) from the Holy Land; "the grid-iron on which the blessed St. Lawrence was roasted;" the very "bread which our Lord Jesus Christ gave to Judas;" some of "the blood of Christ;" some hairs of the Saviour's beard; the iron of the lance with which Longinus pierced his side, "and the blood on it was as fresh as if the deed had just been committed;" "a piece of the sponge with which Jesus Christ, our God, was given gall and vinegar when he was on the cross," and his garments for which the soldiers cast lots, besides relics of saints beyond count. On a stone of many colors were the "tears of the three Marys and of St. John, and these tears looked fresh, as if they had just fallen."

At Trebizond, on the Black Sea, they had already touched on the confines of Timur's dominions, for the prince of that place paid tribute to the Emperor. "The arms which Timur Beg bears," says Clavijo, "are three circles like O's, drawn in this manner, ⁘, and this is to signify that he is lord of the three parts of the world. He ordered this device to be stamped on his coins, and that those who are tributary to him shall have it stamped on the coins of their countries." It was of the greatest benefit to the Spanish envoys to travel in the company of Timur's own ambassador. After many adventures they reached Teheran, and from here to Samarkand they were forwarded by post-horses, which were maintained by the Emperor on all the principal routes; and they were entertained and cared for by the governors of towns and villages. Their journey through Persia was in the heats of July, and many of the party succumbed and died, what with the heat, the dust, the lack of water, and the great pace at which their post-horses travelled; for Timur "is better pleased with him who travels a day and a night for fifty leagues, and kills two horses, than with him who does the distance in three days."

"Timur, considering that the leagues were very long in his empire of Samarkand, divided each league into two, and placed small pillars on the road to mark each league, ordering all his followers to march at least ten of these leagues on each day's journey; and each of these leagues was equal to two leagues of Castile. . . . And they do not only travel the distance which the lord has ordered, but sometimes fifteen or twenty leagues in a day and night."

Fancy a whole kingdom in which each official is forced to travel *at least* sixty miles per day, whether he likes or not!

"When we arrived at any city or village, the first thing was to ask for the chief of the place; and they took the first man they met in the street, and with many blows forced him to show the house of the chief. The people who saw them coming, and knew they were the troops of Timur Beg, ran away as if the devil was after them; and those who were behind their shops shut them up and fled, crying '*Elchee!*' which means ambassador; and saying that with the ambassadors there would come a black day for them."

And, in fact, the villagers had to furnish all that the travellers required, and if any one failed he was killed, or, at the least, beaten; "and thus it was that the people were in marvellous terror of the lord and of his servants."

"With these people Timur has performed many deeds and conquered in many battles; for they are a people of great valor, excellent horsemen, expert with the bow, and enured to hardships. If they have food, they eat; and if not, they suffer cold and heat, hunger and thirst, better than any people in the world. . . . They do not leave their women, children, and flocks behind when they go to the wars, but take all with them."

They are, says a writer quoted by Vámbéry, "a people who weep at their feasts, but laugh in their battles, who follow their leader blindly, are content with cold and hunger, do not know rest or pleasure, have not even words to express them in their language. They prepare and carry their own arms, are animated by one soul and one spirit, not dainty in food or clothes, unpitying, ready to tear the unborn child from its mother."

They despised the life of towns, and held agriculture fit for slaves. They were not willing to subsist on "the top of a weed," as they called wheat. Since the time of Chengiz-Khan, every soldier had his appointed place in war—in the right wing, the left wing, or the centre; and these places were handed down from father to son.

"We met many of them, and they were so burned by the sun that they looked as if they had come out of hell."

On the 31st of August, 1404, the ambassadors reached the neighborhood of Samarkand. They were kept waiting for eight days before they had audience; "for it is the custom not to see any ambassador until five or six days are passed, and the more important the ambassador may be, the longer he has to wait." Finally they were presented.

"Timur Beg was seated in a portal, at the entrance to a beautiful palace, and he was sitting on the ground. Before him there was a fountain, which threw up the water very high, and in it were some red apples. The lord was seated cross-legged, on silken embroidered carpets, amongst round pillows. He was dressed in a robe of silk, with a high white hat on his head, on the top of which was a ruby, with pearls and precious stones about it."

They were very well received, and given an honorable place above the ambassador from China. Timur asked after the King of Spain. "How is my son, the King? These Franks are truly a great people, and I will give my benediction to the King of Spain, my son, who lives at the end of the world." Here, then, at the court of Timur, were met ambassadors from the two extremities of the habitable globe—China and Spain.

Banquets followed, with profusion of meats, boiled and roasted, and with fruits of all kinds, and drink out of golden jugs; and later on drinking-bouts at which the Emperor's wives were present, unveiled. These took place under magnificent tents of silk, embroidered with gold and gems.

"There were gold tables, each standing on four legs, and the tables and legs were all in one. And seven golden vials stood upon them, two of which were set with large pearls, emeralds, and turquoises, and each one had a ruby near the mouth. There were also six round golden cups—one set with large pearls inside, and in the centre of it was a ruby two fingers broad, and of a brilliant hue."

Their interpreter was late in bringing them to this feast, and Timur was very angry.

"How is it that you have caused me to be enraged and put out? Why were you not with the Frank Ambassador? I order that a hole be bored through your nose; that a rope be passed through it, and that you be dragged through the army, as a punishment."

"He had scarcely finished speaking, when men took the interpreter by the nose to bore a hole in it."

It is satisfactory to know that the wretch escaped by the intercession of the officer who attended on the Spanish envoys. As they had not eaten freely, the Emperor sent to their lodgings "ten sheep and a horse to eat, and also a load of wine, and dressed the ambassadors in robes, and gave them shirts and hats."

There was great feasting, for some of Timur's grandsons were to be married; and another grandson, Pir Muhammad, ruler of India, was present. The profusion and magnificence of these feasts impressed the ambassadors, and they seem to have been chiefly struck with the splendid tents and pavilions of silk, built like castles, each with a multitude of rooms.

Timur's chief wife was present in "a robe of red silk, trimmed with gold lace, long and flowing. It had no waist, and fifteen ladies held up the skirts of it to enable her to walk. She wore a crested headdress of red cloth, very high, covered with large pearls, rubies, emeralds, and other precious stones, and embroidered with gold lace. On the top of all there was a little castle, on which were three very large and brilliant rubies, surmounted by a tall plume of feathers. . . . Her hair, which was very black, hung down over her shoulders ; and they value black hair much more than any other color. She was accompanied by three hundred ladies," and when she sat down " three ladies held her headdress with their hands, that it might not fall on one side." The other wives were no less gorgeously arrayed.

" On this day they had much entertainment with the [fourteen] elephants, making them run with horses and with the people, which was very diverting ; and when they all ran together it seemed as if the earth trembled. . . . In this horde which the lord had assembled there were as many as fourteen or fifteen thousand tents, which was a beautiful thing to see."

So with feastings every day the mission was entertained, and was finally dismissed with honorable presents. The ambassadors returned over nearly the same route by which they had come, and arrived at the Spanish court on the 24th day of March, 1406, after an absence of about three years.

Their narrative is valuable, in that it gives a truthful though a dull picture of the court of the great warrior King. It is at the same time most disappointing, in that we fail to gain that vivid, life-like impression of his personality which they might have given. Perhaps the most striking idea to be obtained from it is that the intellectual superiority of the envoys to the Moguls (which we unthinkingly and at once assume) is less marked than one might have expected. Timur's officers do not seem especially rude and ignorant as compared with the Spanish gentlemen. Timur's court was not a mere assembly of his officials. It was organized in a fashion as orderly as that of the Spanish King. Special ranks had special privileges. A Tarkhan, for example, had *les grandes entrées;* the mace-bearers could not stop him. A more extraordinary accompaniment of this rank was that neither he nor his children could be called to account till their crimes exceeded nine in number; and the title was hereditary. Timur himself was a far more important figure than any of his Western contemporaries. To complete our view of him, it is necessary to consult the narratives of the native historians of India and his own Memoirs. And in these native histories we may leave out of consideration any consecutive account of the mere events of his reign. These events were a long succession of bloody *razzias* on a large scale, all alike in the main. When one is understood, all are.

The Life of Timur, as Told by the Native Historians

The native historians and poets have handed down to us some accounts of the actions and sayings of Chengiz-Khan which accurately describe the military life of Timur. Of Chengiz it is said in verse:

In every direction that he urged his steed
He raised dust commingled with blood.

Here is Chengiz's letter demanding the treasure of Bokhara. It might have been written by Timur to the chief men of any one of his conquered cities, just at that fearful moment when his soldiery were driving the inhabitants like sheep into the surrounding plains till the walls were emptied, and just before the sacking of the town began. The letter concludes thus: "O men of Bokhara! You have been guilty of enormous crimes; hence the wrath of God, of whose vengeance I am the instrument, hath employed me against you. Of all the property in this city which is visible, it would be needless to require an account. What I demand is the immediate surrender of all that is concealed."

The trembling chiefs reveal the sites of the hidden treasures; the soldiers loot and plunder; the wretched populace is herded in the fields; in a few days the number of prisoners becomes troublesome; the artisans and the men of learning are segregated from the rest, and are despatched to people some one of the conqueror's cities—to Kesh or Samarkand; the despairing remnant is divided into tens or twenties, and a Mogul warrior is told off to slaughter them, and to produce at nightfall ten or twenty heads to go towards the building of a horrid monument to commemorate the butchery. After the conquest of Bagdad, one hundred and twenty such pyramids of heads were built. Sometimes they were made by Timur's "engineers," by building the whole body of the victims into the structure with brick and clay and mortar. Two thousand prisoners, not all dead, were the materials of one such monument.

When a city was sacked, the walls were usually levelled to the ground and grain was sowed on the site. The tombs of the saints were spared, and were often embellished and enlarged. The infidels who denied the unity of God and the legation of his prophet were almost invariably slain unless they were artisans. "Half of the garrison had their throats cut; the other half were hurled headlong from the battlements," is one entry of Timur's diary.

After Chengiz-Khan had captured Bokhara the history of his conquest was given in a line by one of the sufferers: "The Mongols came, destroyed, burnt, slaughtered, plundered, and departed." The history of Timur's raids is written in that one sentence. They were all alike.

Here is Timur's own account of a massacre in 1387, which was commemorated by the building of 70,000 human heads into a pyramid plastered with mud:

"I conquered the city of Isfahan, and I trusted in the people of Isfahan, and I delivered the castle into their hands. And they rebelled, and they slew three thousand of the soldiers. And I also commanded a general slaughter of the people of Isfahan."

The condition of an invaded province is described by an earlier writer: "There were many who withered with fear, and a muttering arose, as of a drum beaten under a blanket."

Timur's expedition to India was undoubtedly inspired by the hope of plunder. But his *Memoirs* ("his lying Memoirs," as an English commentator calls them) declare that he was impelled to this invasion in order to obtain the title *ghazi*, victor of infidels and polytheists. He sought counsel of his princes and nobles in the matter. Some urged the invasion for one reason, some for another. Prince Muhammad Sultan favored it on account of the "seventeen" mines situated in India. One of these was a mine of gold, another of iron, and the last "a mine of steel."

Timur's conquest of India laid the foundations of the Mogul Empire, and it is important for that reason chiefly. In its incidents it was a mere raid on an immense scale, like so many of his other campaigns. He passed the Hindu Kush Mountains in the spring of A.D. 1398, and in December he was proclaimed Emperor of Delhi. His path was marked by slaughter and ravage, and for five days Delhi itself was given over to pillage. Fifteen days he remained within its walls, and by March, 1399, he had crossed the borders of India once more, on his way to subdue the Sultan of Turkey, Bajazet, who died a captive in his camp.

While Timur lived the official prayers at Delhi were recited in his name, and at his death in the name of his son.

During Timur's march into India more than one hundred thousand Hindu prisoners had fallen into his hands, and it was feared that they might turn against their captors, to whom they were, at any rate, a serious embarrassment. Timur was advised to put the prisoners to death. "He listened to this considerate and wise advice, and gave orders" to that effect. And accordingly they were all slain "with the sword of holy war." The butchers must have been weary of the slaughter, for it is related that even "one of the chief ecclesiastics, who in all his life had never even slaughtered a sheep, put fifteen Hindus to the sword."

These terrible and immense misfortunes produced in the afflicted nations a universal belief that this was the scourge of God. The fatalistic side of Islam exactly expresses this state of acquiescence in overwhelming misfortune. The passage following might have been written of Timur, though, in fact, it refers to another:

"At the time when the page of creation was blank, and nothing had yet taken form or shape, the Supreme Wisdom, with a view to preserve regularity and order in the world, fixed the destiny of each man, and deposited the key for unravelling each difficulty in the hands of an individual endowed with suitable talents. A time was fixed for everything, and when that time comes all obstacles are removed [from his career]."

Though Timur has left Memoirs which are written as if by himself, they are probably the work of his officers, revised by the Emperor. It is said that his secretaries recorded every important event, as is usual in the East, and that he caused their records to be read over to him, correcting them from moment to moment, either by his own recollections, or by the evidence of eye-witnesses to the scenes described. The Moguls of Timur's day used the alphabet introduced by Nestorian missionaries. A century later the Emperor Babar invented a special character for the Turki language.

Timur traces his lineage to Abu-al-Atrak, —the "Father of the Turks,"—the son of Japhet. The great-great-grandfather of Timur was the prime-minister (so to say) of Zagatai, son of Chengiz-Khan. The immaculate conception of Alan Koua, the common ancestress of Chengiz and of Timur, was an article of faith in his court.

His father, Turghai, was the chief of the tribe of Berlas, and the ruler of the city of Kesh, where Timur was born. While he was still a young man, during his father's lifetime, he was a successful commander of 1,000 men. After the death of his father and of his patron Amir Kazghan of Transoxania, his fortunes were at a low ebb. He was obliged to fly to the desert for safety. He tells us that frequently he could command no more than 100 followers, and very often he had but one or two. Still, he was always the chief of his tribe and therefore important; his adherents were brave, of good birth, and enterprising. His own account of the rise in his fortunes gives a picture worth recording.

"I had not yet rested from my devotions when a number of people appeared afar off; and they were passing along in a line with the hill.* I mounted my horse and came behind them, that I might know their condition, and what men they were. They were in all seventy horsemen; and I asked of them, saying, 'Warriors, who are ye?' and they answered unto me, 'We are the servants of Amir Timur, and we wander in search of him, and lo! we find him not.' And I said, 'I also am one of his servants. How say ye if I bring you where he is?' And one of them put his horse to speed, and carried news to the three leaders saying, 'We have found a guide who can lead us to Amir Timur.' The leaders gave orders [to bring the guide]. When their eyes fell upon me, they were overwhelmed with joy, and they alighted and they came, and they kneeled, and they kissed my stirrup. I also alighted and took them in my arms. And I put my turban on the head of [one]; and my girdle on [another]; and I clothed [another] with my cloak. And they wept, and I wept also. When the hour of prayer was arrived, we prayed together; and I made a feast."

This is very like the Iroquois. It might be Uncas and Chingacook. And after the feast they were all ready to harry, slay, burn, torture, to steal cattle, and to fight or run away, as served best. Such was his early fortune.

"He was of good stature, fair complexion, an open countenance, and he had a shrill voice." His descendant, the Emperor Jahangir, tells us that there was no authentic portrait of him in his time. A famous etching of Rembrandt's (No. 270) seems to me to express his character—force, patience, craft—exactly; just as another of Rembrandt's etchings (No. 289) might serve for a portrait of Chengiz-Khan. It is almost certain that he was illiterate, and that his Memoirs are not written by his own hand, though undoubtedly they are often in his very words. One of his firmans was signed with the imprint of his hand in red ink. All of them might have been signed in blood. The famous anecdote of the ant does duty in a Persian life of Timur. "I was once forced," he says, "to take shelter from my enemies in a ruined building. To divert my mind from my hopeless condition, I fixed my eyes on an ant, which was carrying a grain of wheat up a high wall. Sixty-nine times it fell to the ground, but the insect persevered, and the seventieth time it reached the top. The sight gave me courage at the moment, and I never forgot the lesson."

Early in his career (in 1370) Timur admitted Amir Seiyid Berrekah, the most distinguished of the Prophet's descendants (Ali was his ancestor) into his camp, and restored to him the revenues devoted to the shrines and to religious uses. A friendship, which seems to have been warm and sincere, sprang up between the holy man and the warrior and endured till the death of the Seiyid. The cautious policy of Timur's earlier years may have resulted from this companionship. His profuse professions of devotion to Islam are no doubt due to it. Timur was of the sect of Ali—a Shia. I have not been able to trace when his descendants assumed the Sunni faith; but Babar (1500) declares that in his time the inhabitants of Samarkand were all orthodox Sunnis.

Timur's Maxims of Government

Timur laid down twelve maxims of government, and the following paragraphs are selected from this part of his institutes. No doubt these are also his very words in many cases.

"Persons of wisdom and deliberation and vigilance and circumspection, and aged men endowed with knowledge and foresight, I admitted to my private councils; and I associated with them, and I reaped benefit and acquired experience from their conversation. The soldier and the [civilian] subject I regarded with the same eye. And such was the discipline among my troops and my subjects that the one was never injured or oppressed by the other."

"From among the wise and prudent who merited trust and confidence, who were worthy of being consulted on the affairs of government, and to whose care I might submit the secret concerns of my empire, I selected a certain number whom I constituted the repositories of my secrets; and my weighty and hidden transactions, and my secret thoughts and intentions I delivered over to them."

"By the *wazirs*, and the secretaries, and the scribes, I gave order and regularity to my public councils; I made them the keepers of the mirror of my government, in which they showed unto me the affairs of my empire and the concerns of my armies and my people; and they kept rich my treasury; and they secured plenty and prosperity to my soldiers and to my subjects; and by proper and skilful measures they repaired the disorders incident to empire; and they kept in order the revenues and the expenses of government; and they exerted themselves in promoting plenty and population throughout my dominions."

"Men learned in medicine and skilled in the art of healing, and astrologers, and geometricians, who are essential to the dignity of empire, I drew around me; and by the aid of physicians and surgeons I gave health to the sick; and with the assistance of astrologers I ascertained the benign or malevolent aspect of the stars, their motions, and the revolution of the heavens; and with the aid of geometricians and architects I laid out gardens, and planned and constructed magnificent buildings."

"Historians and such as were possessed of information and intelligence I admitted to my presence; and from these men I heard the lives of the prophets and patriarchs, and the histories of ancient princes, and the events by which they arrived at the dignity of empire, and the causes of the declension of their fortunes; and from the narratives and the histories of those princes, and from the manners and conduct of each of them I acquired experience and knowledge; and from those men I heard the descriptions and the traditions of the various regions of the globe, and acquired knowledge of the situations of the kingdoms of the earth."

"To travellers and to voyagers of every country I gave encouragement, that they might communicate unto me the intelligence and transactions of the surrounding nations; and I appointed merchants and chiefs of caravans to travel to every kingdom and to every country that they might bring unto me all sorts of valuable merchandise and rare curiosities from . . . Hindustan and from the cities of Arabia . . . and from the islands of the Christians, that they might give me information of the situation and of the manners and of the customs of the natives and inhabitants of those regions, and that they might observe and communicate unto me the conduct of the princes of every kingdom and every country towards their subjects."

Timur's instructions for collecting the revenue are very full. The paragraphs following will give an idea of their form.

"And I commanded that the Amirs

. . . should not, on any account, demand more than the taxes and duties established. And to every province . . . I ordained that two supervisors should be appointed; that one of them should inspect the collections and watch over the concerns of the inhabitants, that they might not be impoverished, and that the [*over-lord*] might not ill-use or oppress them, . . . and that the other supervisor should keep a register of the public expenses, and distribute the revenues among the soldiers."

"And I ordained that the collection of the taxes from the subject might, when necessary, be enforced by menaces and by threats, but never by whips and by scourges. The governor whose authority is inferior to the power of the scourge is unworthy to govern. I ordained that the revenue and taxes should be collected in such a manner as might not be productive of ruin to the subject or of depopulation to the country." *

* One-third of the gross produce of the cultivated land was the share of the government, and so remained under his descendants in India.

"And I ordained that if the rich and the powerful should oppress the poorer subject and injure or destroy his property, an equivalent for damage sustained should be levied upon the rich oppressor and be delivered to the injured person, that he might [thus] be restored to his former estate."

"I appointed a *Suddur*, a man of holiness and of illustrious dignity, to watch over the conduct of the Faithful; that he might regulate the manners of the times; and appoint superiors in holy offices; and establish in every city and in every town, a judge of penetration, and a doctor learned in the law, and a supervisor of the markets, of the weights and the measures."

"And I established a judge for the army, and a judge for the subjects; and I sent into every province and kingdom an instructor in the law, to deter the Faithful from those things which are forbidden and to lead them in the truth."

"And I ordained that in every town and in every city there should be founded a mosque, and a school, and a monastery, and an alms-house for the poor and indigent, and a hospital for the sick and infirm, and that a physician should be appointed to attend the hospital; and that in every city a government-house and a court for the administration of justice should be built; and that superintendents should be appointed to watch over the cultivated lands, and over the husbandmen."

"And I commanded that they should build places of worship and monasteries in every city; and that they should erect structures for the reception of travelers on the high roads and that they should make bridges across the rivers."

"And I commanded that the ruined bridges should be repaired; and that bridges should be constructed over the rivulets and over the rivers; and that on the roads, at the distance of one stage from each other, caravansaries should be erected; and that guards and watchmen should be stationed on the road, and that in every caravansary people should be appointed to reside; and that the watching and guarding of the roads should appertain unto them ; and that those guards should be answerable for whatever should be stolen on the roads from the unwary traveller."

"And I ordered that the *Suddur* and the judge should, from time to time, lay before me the ecclesiastical affairs of my empire ; and I appointed a judge in equity, that he might transmit unto me all civil matters of litigation that came to pass among my troops and my subjects."

In these maxims and regulations we have a picture which, if it stood by itself, would portray an enlightened monarch, severe, perhaps, but not without benevolence. There is nothing in these paragraphs that might not have been written by Louis XIV. of France, for example, as a guide to his governors of Dauphiné or of Languedoc. Hard as was the fate of the French peasant of that time under the semi-feudal rule of his various overlords, we know that it was freedom itself compared to the condition of Timur's subjects. How then are we to reconcile these liberal-minded maxims with the known facts ?

In the first place, we must remember that the *Memoirs* of Timur were written late in his life, when he desired to leave a memorial of himself which might serve to equal him to the most intelligent of the kings and sultans whom he had overthrown. Bagdad and Damascus were seats of learning and magnificence when he destroyed them. The mosques and colleges which he erected in Samarkand were no unworthy rivals of the edifices of those great cities. The ruler of Samarkand desired to be remembered along with the great Caliphs as a wise King and a patron of learning. This desire led him to throw a certain glamour over all his actions. Moreover, he had a high reverence for the laws of Chengiz-Khan, and he desired to leave behind him a code of the same sort, which should be reverenced by his own successors.

He is even accused, by one of the historians, with valuing the laws of Chengiz above the Kuran, and in many ways his practice proves that the charge was true. The political ideal of Chengiz-Khan was the formation of a military state, whose power should be centralized in the King. He lived long enough to realize this, in great measure, and to show his successors that it was possible to weld scores of individual tribes into something like a nation. In Timur's day the theoretic basis of the State was the law of the Kuran. Timur's professions of Islam were loud; he was a zealous builder of mosques, and a prompt paymaster of religious tithes. But in all matters of State he was guided by the laws of Chengiz, not by those of Muhammad. The Muhammadan maxim, *All Muslims are brethren*, makes nationality unimportant, or even impossible, as has often been pointed out. Timur never permitted a theory like this to interfere with immemorial usage, which was the basis of the laws of Chengiz-Khan. I suppose that the mass of his followers thought very little about religion of any kind, and were loyal to the King from fear of punishment and from hope of plunder.

In the second place Timur *was*, in his own way and in his own day, a supremely wise

King. He had been one of the greatest of military commanders, but he had also "learned the incalculable advantage which wisdom has over force," and experience had taught him that the civilian subject must not be pressed more than so much, and that so much was enough to provide for the wants of his armies, and for the splendor of his government. It is impossible to believe that he was inspired by a sincere desire for the good of the husbandman, like one of his descendants; but it is beyond a doubt that a long experience in governing had demonstrated to him that the subject must have something like fixity of tenure in his property, if the taxes were to come in with regularity. His administration was modelled on what he had observed in Persia, in Syria, in Turkey. His maxims are very nearly such as would have been written by any good Muslim like his friend the Seiyid Berekah. They are by no means the outcome of original thinking. They show, rather, how much of the practical wisdom of his predecessors in the ancient monarchies of the East could be appreciated, at least theoretically, by the descendant of Turki shepherds. Appreciated, these maxims were, since they are set down in the *Memoirs*. Appropriated, as a practical code of laws for all his dominions, they were not.

Again, we must recollect that the enlightenment of his empire was confined to a very few cities, and the learning to a very small number of doctors of the law and men of science. The military chiefs were profoundly illiterate and rude,* though they were very

* The culture of the Arabs had, however, begun to penetrate the higher ranks, and the following anecdote is very interesting in showing how the old and the new ideals of conduct were blended : In the pursuit of the Sultan of Bagdad (Ahmed Khan, A.D. 1403), two of Timur's officers were perishing from thirst. They could only find two small pots of water. Aibaj Oghlan drank one, and declared to his companion, Jelalhamid, that he should die if he did not have the other also. Jelal recalled a tale of a Persian similarly circumstanced who had said to his Arab companion: "The generosity of the Arabs is so famous that it has become proverbial everywhere. It would be a great proof of this truth if, to save me from certain death, you should give me your water also." To maintain the reputation of his race the Arab gave up his share of the water. Jelal went on to say : "I wish to imitate the Arab, and I will give you the water on condition that you will make known to the princes of your house this sacrifice ; so that the

much above the tribesmen. The tribesmen do not seem to have been superior to the Huron Indians, as we-know them by the Jesuit *Relations*, for example. The cultivated land was of relatively small extent. The vast majority of the people were shepherds, and they have changed but little to this day wherever they have been left to themselves. It is only when they have come under the influence of superior races, as in China or in Hindustan, that they have taken on even a shade of culture.

Timur's regulations referred theoretically, perhaps, to vast areas of his empire. It is certain, however, that they were nowhere enforced in the enlightened way suggested in these *Memoirs* ("these lying Memoirs"),

---

memory of this deed may always redound to the credit of the descendants of Jagatai Khan and be cited as a proof of my courage to all our descendants." Whereupon Jelal gave up his share. It is a pleasure to record that he did not die.

The tales of Boccaccio (1350) show that the Italians of that day held the Arabs to be their teachers in chivalry, and at least their equals in art, in science, in civilization. The essence of this story, so it seems to me, is that Arab chivalry had also become the highest ideal of the Mogul chiefs of 1403—of the rude and violent descendants of *Jagatai*.

and that they were in practical effect only along the main roads and in the immediate vicinity of the larger towns and cities. The Spanish ambassadors testify that the people were in "marvellous terror" of Timur and his servants.

If we understand the *Memoirs* in this light they are of great importance. It is of immense interest to know that this absolute ruler even cared to appear to posterity as an enlightened King. It is clear that Timur had reflected profoundly on what he had been told by the wise men of his court and on what he had himself observed in foreign lands which were far beyond his own in culture. Great as was his genius and success as a Captain, we are forced to give an equal admiration to his intelligence as a Ruler. The maxims of his government were household words in the courts of the Emperors, his descendants; but their methods, though peremptory enough, were gentle compared to his.

One of them—Akbar—two hundred years later actually carried out these regulations in practical form, and Akbar's fame as a great King is forever secure for this reason alone.

Timur's family affections were ardent and devoted. On his campaigns he was accompanied by his wives and children to long distances from Samarkand. In 1382 his favorite daughter died, and he sank into a melancholy so deep and persistent as to threaten serious danger to the State, whose affairs he totally neglected. The death of his eldest sister and of a favorite wife in 1383 affected him profoundly. He gave himself up to grief, and neglected all business till his attention was imperatively called for. He was fond of his sons and proud of them; yet he ruled them with an iron rule. It is recorded that on occasions the princes, grown men and sturdy warriors, were subjected to the bastinado like the meanest of his slaves.

The Persian poet Hafiz was a contemporary of Timur's, and there is an anecdote of their meeting.* One of the *ghazels* declares that if this Turk would accept his homage,

* Hafiz died, however, four years before the capture of Shiraz.

—For the black mole on his cheek
I would give the cities of Samarkand and Bokhara.

Timur upbraided him for this verse, and said: "By the blows of my well-tempered sword I have conquered the greater part of the world in order to enlarge Samarkand and Bokhara, my capitals and residences; and you, pitiful creature, would exchange these two cities for a mole." "O Sovereign of the world," said Hafiz, "it is by similar acts of generosity that I have been reduced, as you see, to my present state of poverty." It is reported that the monarch was appeased by the witty answer, and that the poet departed with magnificent gifts.

A less likely tale is told of a jest of the poet Kermani, who, with other wits, was in the bath with Timur. The King asked the poet, "What price wouldst thou put on me if I were for sale?" "About five-and-twenty *aspers*," said Kermani. "Why, that is about the price of the sheet I have on," rejoined Timur. "Well, of course I meant the sheet, for thou alone art not worth a farthing."

Timur's *Memoirs* recite a few cases in

which he was merciful to the rulers or to the inhabitants of a city; these are usually in the early portions of his career, before his power was consolidated, and it is never certain that his mercy was not policy. He is always proud of the valor of his own troops, but it is not recorded that he was in the least tender or careful of them, except upon one occasion. He was returning from India with his spoils. "There was a river in the way, over which I crossed and encamped. Some of the sick men were drowned in crossing the river, so I directed that all my own horses and camels should be used for transporting the sick and feeble. On that day all my camp crossed the river." He was always profuse in his rewards to the survivors. He does not lament the dead in his own army, and, indeed, there is no reason why a good Muslim should do so.

Early in his career Timur discovered, he says, "the incalculable advantage which wisdom has over force, and with what small means the greatest designs may be accomplished." He never forgot the lesson. He was no braver leader, hardly more skilled, than his Amirs; but he was more crafty, more patient, more constant, and of absolutely indomitable will.

His relation to his chiefs is well shown in the following extract from the *Memoirs*:

"*Timur Instructs the Princes and Amirs about the Conduct of the War*

"I now held a Court; I issued a summons to the princes, *amirs*, commanders of thousands, of hundreds, and to the braves of the advance-guard. They all came to my tent. All my soldiers were brave veterans, and had used their swords manfully under my own eyes. But there were none who had seen so many fights and battles as I had seen, and no one who could compare with me in the amount of fighting I had gone through, and the experience I had gained.* I therefore gave them instructions as to the mode of carrying on war; on making and

* This refers to the year 1398 in India. Timur was then sixty-two years old.

meeting attacks; on arraying their men; on giving support to each other; and on all the precautions to be observed in war. . . . When I had finished [they] testified their approbation, and carefully treasuring up my counsel, they departed, expressing their blessings and thanks."

Before setting out on an important campaign, Timur personally attended to the equipment and provisioning of his army. Supplies and forage were collected and stored. Each soldier was directed to furnish himself with a bow, thirty arrows, and a water-bag. Every ten men had, in common, a tent, two mattocks, a spade, a shovel, a sickle, a saw, a hatchet, a rope, a cooking-kettle, one hundred needles, an awl, besides the necessary riding and baggage animals. The equipment seems to be modest, except as to the supply of needles; but the enumeration (from Price's Muhammadan History) omits the sword and buckler, the mace, the spear, the javelin, with which many soldiers were certainly provided; and says nothing of the leather jerkins lined with iron, of the helmets, or of the quilted cuirass for man and horse. The representation of two warriors fighting, used on the cover of this book, is copied from a Persian miniature of about Timur's day.

The armies themselves were immense. Two hundred thousand skilled warriors were assembled for the conquest of China. At a review of his troops in Persia the front of the army covered more than seventeen miles. Irregular troops flocked to his standards in the hope of plunder. Thousands and thousands of camp-followers and prisoners were charged with the transportation and the collection of forage. His Mogul warriors were like the Afghans of Sultan Bahlol, "they knew only to eat and how to die." Their savagery is exactly that of the red Indian. To defile a Hindu sanctuary they filled their boots with the blood of the sacred cows and poured it over the idol. "Vanquished they ask no favor; vanquishing they show no mercy."

"My principal object in coming to Hindustan [says Timur] and in undergoing all this toil and hardship was to accomplish two things. The first was to war with infidels, the enemies of the Muhammadan religion; and by this religious warfare to acquire some claim to reward in the life to come. The other was a worldly object, that the army of Islam might gain something by plundering the wealth of the infidels: plunder in war is as lawful as their mothers' milk to Musulmans who fight for their faith, and the consuming of that which is lawful is a means of grace."

This definition of the means of grace sounds like a distorted reminiscence of his friendship with the Seiyid Berrekah.

"I have not been able [he said] to effect my vast conquests without some violence and the destruction of a great number of true believers; but I am now resolved to perform a good and great action, which shall be an expiation of all my sins. I mean to exterminate the idolaters of China. And you, my dear companions, who have been the instruments of many of my crimes, shall share in the merit of this great work of repentance." Fortunately for the infidels of

China, he died at the very beginning of this enterprise.

In nearly two-score campaigns Timur overran many kingdoms and tribes. "He annihilated empires as one tears up grass." He penetrated Siberia till his camps were nearly fifteen hundred miles distant from Samarkand. His forces ravaged southeastern and southern Russia to the Don and the Sea of Azof. His invasions of India carried him to Delhi and beyond. Georgia, Anatolia, Armenia and Syria were conquered, and the great cities of Smyrna, Aleppo, Bagdad, and Damascus were destroyed. He was just beginning a campaign against China when he died, three hundred miles east of Samarkand (A. D. 1405).

Such amazing military successes imply genius of the first order, and of themselves justify his title—"the great."

It cannot be said that he ruled the vast extent of conquered country; but he ravaged all of it, and continued to receive tribute from a great part; from the Persian Gulf to the Caspian, and from the Euxine to the

Ganges, the coins bore his device of overlordship, and tribute and presents enriched his treasury.

Timur had instructed his scribes to record whatever he should say, "even to the last moment of my existence." The injunction was carried out to the letter, for one manuscript of his *Memoirs* ends thus: "At night [March 19, A. D. 1405] calling upon the name of Allah, I lost my senses and resigned my pure soul to the Creator." His pure soul!

Thoroughly to realize the gulf which then separated the East and the West, we have but to recall a single date—our English Chaucer was buried in Westminster Abbey in October, A. D. 1400.

CHAPTER II

ZEHIR-ED-DIN MUHAMMAD BABAR, THE CONQUEROR, EMPEROR OF HINDUSTAN (BORN A.D. 1482, DIED 1530)

THE *Memoirs* of Babar begin with these words: "In the month of Ramazan and in the twelfth year of my age I became King of Ferghana. The country of Ferghana is situated in the fifth climate, on the extreme boundary of the habitable world. On the east it has Kashgar and on the west Samarkand. The revenues of Ferghana may suffice, without oppressing the country, to maintain three or four thousand troops. It is a country of small extent, abounding in grain and fruits"—and of these fruits the melon is the favorite and the chief. To his dying day Babar remembered the melons of his native country. Ferghana was famous for its learned doctors of the law and

HUMAYUN BABAR
JAHANGIR AKBAR

for its poets, too, as we shall see. It was one of the innumerable small states into which Timur's possessions had been divided after his death. This state had fallen to the share of Babar's father, "a prince of high ambitions," a strict Muhammadan, a patron of learning, a poet, and a friend of poets. His favorite poem was the famous *Shah-nameh* of Firdausi, that chronicle of knightly deeds.

He was renowned for his justice; and Babar gives a striking instance of it. A caravan from Northern China had perished in the snow near his capital, at a time when he was in real want. In spite of his necessities the merchandise was sacredly preserved till, after one or two years, the heirs of the merchants came to his city and received it, untouched, from his hands. "His generosity was large," says Babar, "and so was his whole soul; he was of an excellent temper, affable and sweet in his conversation, yet brave, withal, and manly."

On his sudden death, Babar, his eldest son, sixth in descent from Timur, succeeded to the sovereignty, which he was, however, obliged to dispute with his rival brothers and to protect from external foes. Babar's mother was the daughter of Yunis-Khan, a direct descendant of Chengiz-Khan, thirteenth in the male line. "She accompanied me in most of my wars and expeditions." His maternal grandmother was a woman of extraordinary force and wise in counsel. "There were few of her sex who excelled her in sense and sagacity." These women were Babar's guides and counsellors in the small wars with which his early years were occupied. His *Memoirs* are a recital of hundreds of petty combats, sieges, and stratagems, "excursions and alarums," successes and defeats, in the struggle to retain Ferghana or to capture Samarkand. Babar succeeded to the throne about two years before the discovery of America by Columbus, and four years before Vasco da Gama reached India. Ferdinand and Isabella in Spain, Henry VII and Henry VIII in England, were his contemporaries.

Babar's *Memoirs* were written with his own hand in the Turki language, and have come down to us practically unchanged.

They cover nearly all of his history to within a year of his death. All of this history is recounted in the most straightforward simple, engaging, manly way. "I have no intention," he says, "in what I have written, to reflect on any one. All that I have said is only the plain truth. And I have not mentioned it with the least design to praise myself. I have in every word most scrupulously followed the truth. Let the reader, therefore, excuse me."

Babar's father had cherished an overpowering ambition to capture Samarkand, the ancient capital of Timur's kingdom, and Babar succeeded to the desire. During Timur's lifetime the government of the capital had been conferred on one of his sons, and on a grandson. At Timur's death, his youngest son Shahrokh Mirza, the ruler of Khorassan, had seized the city, and had given it over to be ruled by his son Ulugh Beg Mirza, the famous astronomer; "from whom it was taken," says Babar, "by his son Abdul-latif Mirza, who, for the sake of the enjoyments of this fleeting world, murdered his own father, an old man so illustrious for his knowledge.

Ulugh Beg, the ocean of learning and science,
Who was the protector of this lower world,
Drank from Abbas the honey of martyrdom.

Yet his son did not retain the diadem above five or six months;

—Ill does sovereignty become a parricide;
But should he gain it, let six months be the limit of his reign.

The verses are Babar's own.

"After Abdul-latif Mirza,* Abdullah Mirza mounted the throne, and reigned nearly two years. After him the government was seized by Sultan Abusaid Mirza, who conferred it upon his eldest son Sultan Ahmed Mirza. On his death (1494) Sultan Mahmud Mirza ascended the throne, and after him, Baiesanghar Mirza. I took it from Baiesanghar Mirza. The events that followed will be mentioned in the course of these *Memoirs*."

* There is a legend that Ulugh Beg, finding that the stars fore told his assassination at the hands of his son, drove the latter into rebellion by unmerited ill-treatment. But Babar's view of the case is plainly different; and it would seem that Babar should know. See also Vámbéry's *History of Bokhara*, Chapter XII.

The succession of rulers presents a vivid idea of the unsettled period in which Babar lived. Another striking instance may be given. He had five sisters; and two of the five were captured in war and found places in the harems of his enemies. These were the daughters and sisters of kings.

The *Memoirs* go on to give the names and the characters of the Turki chiefs by whom Babar's cause was supported; and his outspoken judgments allow us to know his own character as well as theirs. One was "a good-humored man, of plain, simple manners, who excelled in singing at drinking parties." Another was "a pious, religious, faithful Muslim, whose judgment and talents were uncommonly good. He was of a facetious turn, and though he could neither read nor write, he had an ingenious and elegant vein of wit." "Another was Mir Ali Dost, who was related to my maternal grandmother. I showed him great favor. I was told that he would be a useful man; but during all the years that he was with me, I cannot tell what service he ever did." "Another was

Amir Omar-Beg. He was a brave, plain, honest man. A son of his is still with me; he is a lazy, idle, good-for-nothing fellow. Such a father to have such a son!"

In this manner Babar runs over the catalogue of his officers and companions, and weighs their qualities, just as the Emperor Marcus Aurelius sums up the character of his associates. Let these further instances suffice.

"Indeed, Ali Shir Beg was an incomparable person. From the time that poetry was first written in our language no man has written so much and so well. He also left excellent pieces of music; excellent both as to the airs themselves and as to the preludes. There is not upon record in our history any man who was a greater patron of men of ingenuity and talent than he." Musicians, painters, and poets alike came under his protection; and he was singular in this, that he had neither wife nor child. "He passed through the world unencumbered." He declined the cares of government, and spent his time in study and composition. The following is his: "*Oh, you who say, 'Do not curse Yazid, for possibly the Almighty may have mercy on him,' I say, if the Lord pardoneth all the evil which Yazid did to the descendants of the Prophet, he will also pardon you who may have cursed him.*"

"Another was Sheikhem Beg. He composed a manner of verses in which both the words and sense are terrifying and correspond with each other. The following is his:

During my sorrows of the night the whirlpool of my sighs bears the firmament from its place;
The dragons of the inundations of my tears bear down the four quarters of the habitable world."

When he repeated these verses, the Mulla said to him: "Are you repeating poetry, or are you frightening folks?"*

* I cannot resist quoting a short poem by Abd-er-Razzak to illustrate a different kind of Oriental exaggeration. He was on the shores of the Persian Gulf in May, 1442, and thus describes the intense heat:

Soon as the sun shone forth from the height of heaven,
The heart of stone grew hot beneath its orb;
The horizon was so much scorched-up by its rays,
That the heart of stone became soft like wax;
The bodies of the fishes, at the bottoms of the fish-ponds,
Burned like the silk which is exposed to the fire;
Both the water and the air gave out so burning a heat
That the fish went away to seek refuge in the fire;
In the plains, hunting became a matter of perfect ease,
For the desert was filled with roasted gazelles.

The chief doctor of the canon law in Ferghana was executed by his enemy. Of him Babar, himself the bravest of men, says: "I have no doubt that he was a saint. What better proof of it than that all his enemies perished in a short while? He was also a very bold man, which is also no mean proof of sanctity. All mankind, however brave they be, have some little anxiety or trepidation about them. He had not a particle of either."

Khosrou Shah was thoroughly hated by Babar, who says that, "For the sake of this fleeting and faithless world, which never was and never will be true to anyone, this thankless and ungrateful man seized the Sultan, a prince whom he himself had reared from infancy to manhood, and whose tutor he had been, and blinded him by lancing his eyes. Every day till the day of judgment may a hundred thousand curses light on the head of that man who is guilty of such black treachery; let every man who hears of this action of Khosrou Shah pour out imprecations upon him; for he who hears of such a deed and does not curse him, is himself worthy to be cursed." Ali Shir's verses may have suggested the form of this passage.

Such were the chiefs by whom Babar was surrounded, and through whom and against whom he had to act. Their followers were brave, but inconstant. Their cities alternately welcomed the straggling army of Babar (which was sometimes no more than two hundred warriors) and rejected it.

Babar learned the art of war in a rough school, and he learned it thoroughly. On one occasion, much plunder was unjustly taken by his men, which he made them give up. "Such was the discipline of my army that the whole was restored without reserve, and before the first watch of the next day was over, there was not a bit of thread or a broken needle that was not restored to its owner." He was one of the first to introduce concerted action of divisions of his army in the place of mad rushes of separate hordes and tribes.

Samarkand, the city of Babar's affections, was thrice taken and lost. He is never tired of dwelling on the perfection of its buildings. "In the whole habitable world there are few cities so pleasantly situated." Its walls were paced out by Babar's order, and found to be five English miles in circuit. "It is, he says, in latitude 39° 37′, longitude 99° 16′." This is the calculation from Ulugh Beg's "tables," the longitude being counted from Ferro. Ulugh Beg (1393–1449) was far better fitted to shine as a man of science than as a king. His short reign of three years was a succession of misfortunes, but his fame as a mathematician and as an astronomer is permanent.

Since the time of the Greek schools of Alexandria, the home of the exact sciences had been, successively, Bagdad, Cordova and Seville, Tangiers and Samarkand; * and it was not until the time of Tycho (1576) that such learning was born in the western peoples. Ulugh Beg was the last of the

---

* It is interesting to know that the new masters of Turkistan—the Russians—have lately established an observatory at Tashkend, four centuries and a half after the establishment of that at Samarkand.

Arabian school. A century and a half before Tycho, he constructed mighty instruments for astronomical observation, and, with the aid of a hundred observers and calculators, he prepared his famous tables of the motions of the planets and his catalogues of stars.

"Ulugh Beg's observatory," says Babar, "was erected on the skirts of the hill of Kolik, and was three stories in height. Not more than seven or eight observatories have been constructed in the world. Among these, one was erected by the Caliph Mamun, another was built by Ptolemy at Alexandria." The college, the baths, the mosques, all call for exceeding praise; even "the bakers' shops are excellent, and the cooks are skilful." The streets of Samarkand were paved, and running water was distributed in pipes. Once more we hear of its excellent melons, and of the wine of Bokhara, one of its dependencies. "When I drank wine at Samarkand, in the days when I had my drinking bouts, I used that wine." It was a learned city, too, and hospitable to poets; and here

Babar acquired and practised the poetic art himself, with no mean skill.

The city was full of noble buildings, mosques, colleges, palaces, built by artisans impressed by Timur, and decorated with mosaics, gilding, and pictures.*

The colleges were full of learned men and students; the court of the kings, with poets and painters. This was the heyday of Turki learning, which blossomed in the midst of ignorance. Not all of the chief men could read and write, however, and the memory was therefore highly cultivated. As one of them said: "When a man has once heard anything, how can he forget it?" "Hilali, the poet, had so retentive a memory that he could recall from thirty to forty thousand

* This was not orthodox for good Muslims. Muhammad says, "The angels do not enter a house in which is a dog, nor that house in which there are pictures;" and in another place, more briefly, "every painter is in hell-fire." The Muslims, like the Jews, were no friends to painting and sculpture; but noble architecture early became a passion with them. After Babar's time the arts and learning rapidly declined in Samarkand, and by the seventeenth century the city was stagnant. On May 14, 1868, the Russians took possession, and the twentieth century may witness a revival of learning in the colleges of Turkistan.

couplets." Such mnemonic feats seem incredible to us moderns, who are used to depend upon the eye and not upon the ear. Yet they are doubtless correctly reported. The *Rig-Veda* contains more than ten thousand verses, and for over two thousand years it was preserved solely by oral traditions, and not one, but thousands of Brahmins could recite it word for word.

An alphabet introduced by Nestorian priests had been employed up to Babar's time, as I have said; but he invented and introduced a new manner of writing—the Babari character—and his presents to great nobles were often copies of his poems, written out by his transcribers. He himself was a great stickler for propriety in composition; and on one occasion he soundly rates his eldest son, Humayun, then the reigning monarch in Kabul, for various literary errors. "In consequence of the far-fetched words you have employed, your meaning is by no means very intelligible. Your spelling is not bad, yet not quite correct. You certainly do not excel in letter-writing. In the future you should write unaffectedly, with clearness, using plain words, which cost less trouble to both writer and reader."

Here is one of Babar's early couplets, written when he was in great distress:

Do thou resign to Fate him who injures thee,
For Fate is a servant that will not leave thee unavenged.

And again:

Let the sword of the world be brandished as it may,
It cannot cut one vein without the permission of Allah!

I have found no faithful friend in the world but my soul;
Except my own heart, I have no trusty confidant.

The period to which this refers was a dark one in Babar's fortunes. He had lost Ferghana, and Samarkand was no longer his.

"For nearly one hundred and forty years Samarkand had been the capital of my family. A foreign robber,* one knew not

* This "foreign robber" was a direct descendant of Chengiz-Khan, and, therefore, a relative of Babar himself, who, however, was no friend to the Mogul tribesmen, but counted himself a Turki. Babar is unjust to this rival Sheibani in his *Memoirs*, as also to another rival, Khosrou Shah. Sheibani Khan was an enterprising and successful soldier, a poet, a scholar in Arabic, Turki, and Persian, a builder of colleges and mosques, and a notable patron of learned men.

whence he came, had seized the kingdom, which dropped from our hands. Almighty Allah now gave me back my plundered and pillaged country." It was lost to him, however, by the issue of a pitched battle. "Such was our situation when I precipitated matters and hurried on the battle;

He who with impatient haste lays his hand on his sword,
Will afterward gnaw that hand with his teeth from regret.

"The cause of my eagerness to engage was, that the stars called the 'eight stars' were on that day exactly between the two armies; and if I had suffered that day to elapse, they would have been favorable to the enemy." And he goes on to say, with the experience of his later years: "These observances were all nonsense, and my precipitation was without the least solid excuse."

This battle lost him his kingdom once more; but he never quite recovered from superstition. Witness the following involved account of his reasons for refusing a battle in India toward the end of his life: "If on that same Saturday I had fought, it is probable that I should have won. But it came into my head that last year I had set out on a New Year's Day, which fell on a Tuesday, and had overthrown my enemy on a Saturday. This year we commenced our march on New Year's Day, which fell on a Wednesday, and if we beat them on a Sunday it would be a (too) remarkable coincidence. On that account I did not march my troops"!

I have now to recount what is, and will doubtless remain, one of the standing puzzles of Babar's history. We shall see that Babar was the soul of outspoken boldness, and that he was not afraid to confess himself in the wrong, nor unwilling to amend. He was skilled in the devices of poetic art, but the very essence of the dramatic power of his *Memoirs* is their flowing naturalness and simplicity. The *Memoirs* continue to about the year 1529, a year before his death. Remembering all this, it is more than strange to find in them two sudden gaps, where the narrative breaks off abruptly, and leaves the hero in the midst of the extremest perils.

The first of these gaps occurs at the end of the year 1502, and the narrative is not resumed until 1504.

Babar is defending a fortress with scarcely more than a hundred men. His enemies arrive, and after a severe fight he is forced to cut his way to the nearest gateway and to fly. Every detail of a most exciting hand-to-hand fight is given, even to the number of arrows that Babar discharged. "A man on horseback passed close to me, fleeing up the narrow lane (of the city). I struck him such a blow on the temples with the point of my sword that he bent over as if ready to fall from his horse, but, supporting himself on the wall of the lane, he did not lose his seat, and escaped with the utmost hazard." Through hand-to-hand fighting like this, Babar escapes, and gains the open country, warmly pursued. His adherents are soon reduced to eight, and presently Babar is fleeing alone. At last only two of the enemy were close to him.

"They gained upon me; my horse began to flag. What was to be done? I had about twenty arrows left. The pursuers did not come nearer than a bowshot, but kept on tracking me." The flight had begun before afternoon prayers, and it was now sunset. His enemies called to him, but he pushed on till about bedtime prayers, when he reached a place where his horse could go no farther. His pursuers swore to him by the Kuran that they wished to do him no harm. He forced them to proceed in front of him out of the glen where they were, towards the road, and they continued marching till the dawn. The next day they lay concealed, with but little food, and only a moment for sleep. After midnight another enemy arrived with the information that Babar's chief rival knew their place of concealment. He had been betrayed by his companions. "I was thrown into a dreadful state of agitation. There is nothing which affects a man with more painful feelings than the near prospect of death. 'Tell me the truth,' I exclaimed, 'if indeed things are about to go with me contrary to my wishes, that I may at least perform my last ablutions.' I felt my strength gone. I rose and went to a corner of the garden. I meditated with myself and said: 'Should a man live a hundred, nay a thousand years, yet at last he——'" So the narrative breaks off.

It is not resumed for two years, when Babar's fortunes had improved vastly. Is it a piece of literary art? Is it to spare him the recital of the successful intrigues by which he drove Khosrou Shah from his kingdom and took his place? Is he ashamed of these intrigues, and is this the reason why he blackens the character of Khosrou, of whom others speak so well? There is no solution.

The first break in the narrative might be taken as an accident if it were not for a second occurrence of the same kind in the year 1508, when Babar was deserted by the very Moguls whom he had seduced from their allegiance to Khosrou Shah, and by all his followers of every rank and description. From this second misfortune Babar rescued himself by desperate fighting and reckless personal valor, as we learn from other sources. The fickle tribesmen deserted their former rulers and attached themselves to his fortunes. The Persians became his allies. The cities opened their gates, and he became the master of Kabul, and Kabul was the stepping-stone to India.

Sheibani, the ancient enemy of Babar, who had usurped his kingdom of Samarkand, came to a violent end. His body was dismembered, and his limbs were sent to different kingdoms. His head was stuffed with hay and sent to the Turkish emperor at Constantinople. His skull, set in gold, was used by the Persian king as a drinking-cup. Babar's allies, the Persians, put fifteen thousand prisoners to the sword. Many of these were of Babar's own race, and this alliance with the Persians did not help him to recover his kingdom, though his worst enemies were overcome by their assistance, and he was thus left free to execute his conquest of Hindustan. Taking aid from the hated *Shias* of Persia could never be approved by the orthodox Turki *Sunnis* of Transoxania.

Herat, too, had fallen into the hands of his allies and relatives, and he made a long stay at their court. At a great feast in Herat, Babar had another occasion to show his simple manners. He records the event thus: " In the course of the feast a roast goose was put down in front of me. As I was ignorant of the mode of carving it, I let it alone. Badia-ez-Zeman Mirza (the head of Babar's family) asked me if I did not like it; I told him frankly that I did not know how to carve it." The court was refined and luxurious, and this was a great feast of Babar's relatives to him as a young man. It cost him a little to confess his ignorance of so simple a thing. But he did not shrink.

The fortunes of this city of Herat—Heri—the *Aria* of the Greek chronicles of Alexander—deserve a chapter, not a brief paragraph. In the time of Chengiz-Khan it was a crowded city, having, with its surrounding country, a population of several hundreds of thousands. After its first siege of A.D. 1222–1223 its inhabitants were spared. A revolt on their part led to the second siege of seven months, and to its capture. For seven days and nights it was devoted to plunder and massacre, and the native historians aver that more than a million persons perished. Whatever the exact number may have been, the Mogul troops did not leave until it was supposed no single inhabitant remained alive. After their departure some three thousand wretched beings assembled amid the ruins. In a few hours a band of two thousand Moguls returned and completed the slaughter, and the remnant perished to a man, save for sixteen miserable creatures who had hidden themselves in sewers, in water-courses, in the dome of the mosque. These finally crept fearfully forth amid the smoking ruins of the great and beautiful city. They were joined by other four and twenty from the surrounding country, and for fifteen years these forty individuals were the only inhabitants of the proudest city of the East, which had counted her children by hundreds of thousands. Herat was rebuilt by Octai Khan about A.D. 1235, and it soon recovered its splendor. In the time of Babar it was the most polite city of the East.

Herat is the soul, of which this world is but the body; and if Khorassan be the bosom of the world, Herat is allowed to be the heart.

This is Babar's account of it:

"The city of Herat abounded with eminent men of unrivalled acquirements, each of whom made it his aim and ambition to carry to the highest perfection the art to which he devoted himself. Among these was the Moulana Abdul-rahman Jami, to whom no person of the period could be compared, whether in respect to sacred or to profane science. His poems are well known. His merits are of too exalted a nature to admit of being described by me; but I have been anxious to bring the mention of his name and an allusion to his excellences into these humble pages for a good omen and a blessing." The following quatrain of Babar's is not out of place here:

Though I am not related to Dervishes,
Yet I am devoted to them heart and soul.
Say not that the state of a Prince is remote from that of a Dervish;
Though a King, I am the Dervish's slave.

Babar enumerates the many wise men,

poets, and musicians who were living in Herat in his youth. Jami was the chief of the poets, but he finds space for short biographies of a dozen others, and for some account of the skilled painters and musicians of the court. Professor Vámbéry, who should be an authority on such matters, declares:*

"Every notion a Muhammadan in Asia or elsewhere possesses (at this day) of culture, refinement, high civilization—in short, of all those qualities now only known to him by name—is derived from the conditions which then (in the times from Timur to Babar) flourished at the courts of Herat and Samarkand." By diligently reading the annals of these alien people, they come to seem almost familiar to us, because we distinguish the underlying note of a common human nature, and almost lose the superficial sense of foreignness. Everything appears so modern that we need to force ourselves to return abruptly to our accustomed standards in order to preserve a right perspective.

* *History of Bokhara*, page 241.

The poets and artists of Herat in 1507 form a group that is almost friendly. To acquire a due perception of their separateness, we must seek for a sharp antithesis. The poems of Ali Shir Beg touch us to-day, but we are forced to recognize that Schubert's B-minor symphony would be mere discord to him.

The incident which follows, shows Babar's estimate of the value of poetry, and exhibits his straightforward simplicity of mind. He says: "During a drinking party the following verse was repeated:

> *What can one do to regulate his thoughts, with a mistress possessed of every blandishment?*
> *Where* you *are, how is it possible for our thoughts to wander to another?*

"It was agreed that everyone should make an extempore couplet to the same rhyme, and·I said:

> *What can be done with a drunken sot like you?*
> *What can be done with one foolish as a she-ass?*

"Before this I had always committed my verse to writing. Now, when I had composed these lines, my mind led me to reflections, and my heart was struck with regret that a tongue which could repeat the sublimest productions should bestow any trouble on such unworthy verses; that it was melancholy that a heart, elevated to nobler conceptions, should submit to occupy itself with these despicable fancies. From this time forward I religiously abstained from satirical or vituperative verses. At the time I had not considered how objectionable the practice was." Later on, we find him translating a religious tract into verse. "I composed every day, on an average, fifty-two couplets."

In a winter's journey to Kabul the army was deeply distressed by snows and storms. Finally they halted at a cave. Babar dug for himself a hole in the snow "as deep as my breast and the size of a prayer-carpet," and sat down in it. "Some desired me to go into the cavern, but I would not go. I felt that for me to be in a warm dwelling and in comfort, while my men were in the midst of snow and drift; for me to be enjoying sleep and ease, while they were in distress;

would be a deviation from that society in suffering which was their due. I continued, therefore, to sit in the drift."

On another of his night marches against the enemy, he ascended a high pass. "Till this time I had never seen the star Soheil—Canopus (which is, indeed, not visible in northern latitudes), but on reaching the top, Soheil appeared below, bright, to the south. I said, 'This cannot be Soheil.' They answered, 'It is, indeed, Soheil.'" The descendant of Ulugh Beg came justly by his knowledge of the stars—even of the stars which he had never seen. How many of our soldiers of to-day would recognize Canopus if they saw it?

In his early youth Babar was shamefaced and modest, and for a long time he used no wine. In later years he caroused with a kind of fierce regularity, and he duly chronicles each of his drinking-bouts. After the battle which gave him India, he made, as he says, "an effectual repentance," which was sincere. He broke all his jewelled golden drinking-cups and gave them to dervishes and the poor, made his store of wine into vinegar, and finally issued a proclamation of his change of life, and humbled himself before Allah.

Let us see how a tyrant dreams. Once when Babar had taken a potion of *bhang*, he fell asleep and has recorded his dream : " While under its influence I visited some beautiful gardens. In different beds the ground was covered with flowers. On the one hand were beds of yellow flowers in bloom ; on the other hand, red flowers were in blossom. In many places they sprung up in the same bed, mingled together, as if they had been flung and scattered abroad. I took my seat on a rising ground to enjoy the view of all the flower-plots. As far as the eye could reach, there were flower-gardens of a similar kind." Recollect that this history was written years after the dream. And then he adds : " In the neighborhood of Peshawer, during the spring, the flower-plots are exquisitely beautiful." Wherever this stern warrior went, he planted flower-gardens and orchards and built places of delight.

A little distance from Kabul, Babar constructed a small cistern of red granite on a site overlooking the city, and engraved on its sides these verses:

Sweet is the return of the new year;
Sweet is the smiling spring;
Sweet is the juice of the mellow grape;
Sweeter far the voice of love.
Strive, oh Babar! to secure the joys of life,
Which, alas! once departed, never more return.

"I directed this fountain to be built around with stone. On the four sides of the fountain a fine platform for resting was constructed on a very neat plan. At the time when the *Arghwan* flowers begin to blow, I do not know that any place in the world is to be compared with it."

From Kabul he made several incursions into India, which were mere raids, and finally he set out on his expedition of conquest, aided by the disaffected nobles of the Penjab. There is no space to relate the complex wars and negotiations, nor to describe the final great battle which gave him Agra, the capital. His armies were the Turki hordes with Indian allies;

—In whose stern faces shined the quenchless fire
That after burnt the pride of Asia.

His success was largely due to the discipline which he was one of the first to introduce. The men were armed with bows and arrows, spears, cimeters, and maces, and a few matchlocks. The siege artillery of that day was clumsy and ponderous. "While the bridge of the Ganges was constructing, Ustād Ali Kuli played his gun remarkably well. The first day he discharged it eight times; the second, sixteen times; and for three or four days he continued firing in the same way. It was called the Victorious Gun, and Ustad Khan was rewarded for his success."

After the capture of Agra, in 1526, the treasure was distributed. Humayun, Babar's eldest son and successor, obtained eighty-seven thousand dollars, besides a palace. His other sons and the emirs received all the way from twenty thousand to seventy-five hundred dollars. "Every merchant, every man of letters, everyone in the army, all my relatives and friends, great and small, had presents in silver and gold, in cloth, in jewels, and in captive slaves." Every man, woman, and child, slave or free, in the country of Kabul, received a silver coin of the value of an English shilling. Babar's lavishness became a proverb.

At the same time the famous diamond was captured. "It is so valuable," says Babar, "that it is valued at half the daily expense of the whole world." *

Babar was thus settled on the throne of India, and had become the founder of an empire. Let us see what the conqueror thought of his conquest.

"Hindustan is a country that has few pleasures to recommend it. The people are not handsome. They have no idea of friendly society. They have no genius, no comprehension of mind, no politeness of manner, no kindness or fellow-feeling, no ingenuity or mechanical invention in planning or executing their handicraft works; no skill or knowledge

* This may have been the stone, *The Ocean of Lustre*, now in the treasury of the Shah of Persia. It was not the *Kohinur*, according to the latest authorities.

in design or architecture ; they have no good horses, no good flesh, no grapes or musk-melons, no ice or cold water, no good food or bread, no (public) baths or colleges, no candles, no torches, not a candle-stick even." "The chief excellency of Hindustan is that it is a large country, and has abundance of gold and silver," and many skilled artisans. In Agra alone, he daily employed 680 mechanics, and he kept 1491 stone-masons busy with his various buildings. In another place he says: "The people of Hindustan, and particularly the Afghans, are a strangely foolish and senseless race, possessed of little reflection and less foresight. They can neither persist in and manfully support a war, nor can they continue in amity and friendship."

His life had been one of incessant activity and strife up to this time. "From the eleventh year of my age onward I have never spent two festivals of the Ramazan in the same place." When he was fourteen years of age he was present at a siege, and complains: "For two months there was nothing but siege operations, and no fine fighting." All his active life he spent in fine fighting or in marching to the fray.

"This day I swam across the River Ganges for amusement. I had previously crossed, by swimming, every river that I had met with, the Ganges alone excepted."

In India he had to contend with secret enemies, as well as with armies in the field.

In Agra, Babar was poisoned through the treachery of his cooks and the carelessness of the taster. "The taster was ordered to be cut to pieces. I commanded the cook to be flayed alive. One of the women was trampled to death by an elephant, the other was shot by a matchlock." Babar recovered. "Thanks be to Allah! I did not fully comprehend before that life was so sweet a thing. The poet says:

Whoever comes to the gates of Death,
Knows the value of Life.

Whenever these awful occurrences pass before my memory, I feel myself involuntarily turn faint. The mercy of Allah has bestowed a new life upon me, and how can my tongue express my gratitude?"

By a singular good fortune, we have two of Babar's letters. One is written to his sons in warning and reproof. The other is to an old and trusted friend in Kabul. The first letter shows that he was disappointed and hurt by the conduct of his children; and the last is an outpouring of the griefs of his inmost heart to his friend. He says: "My solicitude to visit my western dominions (Kabul) is boundless and great beyond expression. I trust in Almighty Allah that the time is near at hand when everything will be completely settled in this country. As soon as matters are brought to that state, I shall, with the permission of Allah, set out for your quarters without a moment's delay. How is it possible that the delights of those lands should ever be erased from the heart? How is it possible to forget the delicious melons and grapes of that pleasant region? They very recently brought me a single musk-melon from Kabul. While cutting it up, I felt myself affected with a strong feeling of loneliness and a sense of my exile from my native country, and I could not help shedding tears." He gives long instructions on the military and political matters to be attended to, and continues without a break: "At the southwest of Besteh, I formed a plantation of trees; and as the prospect from it was very fine, I called it Nazergah (the view). You must there also plant some beautiful trees, and all around sow beautiful and sweet-smelling flowers and shrubs." And he goes straight on: "Syed Kasim will accompany the artillery." After more details of the government, he quotes fondly a little, trivial incident of former days and friends, and says: "Do not think amiss of me for deviating into these fooleries." "I conclude with every good wish."

Towards the end of 1529 Babar's health failed rapidly, and his son Humayun also fell ill. The latter was conveyed to Agra and tenderly cared for, but his life was despaired of. One of Babar's high officers, distinguished for his piety, said to Babar that Almighty Allah might vouchsafe to spare Humayun's life in return for the sacrifice of Babar's most precious possession, and suggested that the great diamond captured at Agra be the offering. "No," said Babar, "my own life is the most precious of my possessions, and I devote it to this end." He three times walked about the dying prince and retired to pray. Returning he exclaimed, "I have borne it away;" and in fact, from that time Babar declined and his beloved son waxed stronger. With his unvarying affection for his family, he besought Humayun to be kind and forgiving to his brothers, and, what is rare in such cases, the admonition was faithfully respected during many trying years. In a short time Death, the sunderer of societies, the garnerer of graveyards, the plunderer of palaces, bore him away to the mercy of Allah, the compassionating, the compassionate, and his son reigned in his stead.

"The grave of Babar is marked by two erect slabs of white marble, and, as is common in the East, the different letters of a part of the inscription indicate the number of the year of the *Hegira* in which the Emperor died. The device, in the present instance, seems to me happy:

> *When in heaven Roozvan asked the date of his death,*
> *I told him that heaven is the eternal abode of Babar Padishah.*

"Near the Emperor his wives and children have been interred, and the garden, which is small, was once surrounded by a wall of marble. A running and clear spring yet waters the fragrant flowers of this cemetery, which is the great holiday resort of the people of Kabul. In front of the grave there is a small but chaste mosque of marble, and an inscription upon it sets forth that it was built in the year 1640, by order of the Emperor Shah Jahan, that poor Muhammadans might here offer up their prayers." *

From the hill which overlooks Babar's tomb there is a noble prospect, and the gardens of the city are in full blossom beneath it. In Babar's own words, "the verdure and flowers render Kabul, in the spring, a very heaven."

* Burnes' *Travels into Bokhara*, quoted by Erskine.

Babar has portrayed his own character in words which every generous heart will understand. He was a gentleman and a soldier—throughghbred. He had prudence, knowledge, energy, ambition, and generosity, and "all the qualities from which nobility derives its name." "Exaltation was written on his forehead." Mr. Erskine, the translator of his *Memoirs*, has summed it up judiciously: "A striking feature in Babar's character is his unlikeness to other Asiatic princes. Instead of the stately, systematic, artificial character that seems to belong to the throne in Asia, we find him natural, lively, affectionate, simple, retaining on the throne all the best feelings and affections of common life. We shall find few princes who are entitled to rank higher than Babar in genius and accomplishment. His grandson Akbar may perhaps be placed above him for profound and benevolent policy. The crooked artifice of Aurangzeb is not entitled to the same distinction. The merit of Chengiz-Khan and of Tamerlane terminates in their splendid conquests, which far excelled the achievements of Babar. But in activity of mind, in the gay equanimity and unbroken spirit with which he bore the extremes of good and bad fortune, in the possession of the manly and social virtues, so seldom the portion of princes, in his love of letters, and his success in the cultivation of them, we shall find no other Asiatic prince who can justly be placed beside him."

Two sayings of Babar's, placed side by side, give the key to all his public actions. "Inspired as I was with an ambition for conquest and for extensive dominion, I would not, on account of one or two defeats, sit down and look idly around me;" and again, "How can any man of understanding pursue such a line of conduct as, after his death, must stain his fair fame? The wise have well called Fame a second existence."

The circumstances of Oriental and of Western life are totally dissimilar. "Between us and them crawls the nine-times-twisted stream of Death." If we can make the needed allowances for these differences of time and circumstance, Babar will appear not unworthy to be classed with the great Cæsar as a general, as an administrator, as a man of letters. His character is more lovable than Cæsar's, and reminds us of Henry IV of Francc and Navarre. He conquered India and founded a mighty empire. Take him for all in all, he was the most admirable of the Mogul kings.

THE TOMB OF HUMAYUN

CHAPTER III

HUMAYUN, EMPEROR OF HINDUSTAN (A. D. 1530–1556)—THE ADVENTURES OF FOUR BROTHERS

"*When Fortune's adverse, minds are perverse.*"—PERSIAN SAYING.

THE intelligent Bernier, in his recital of the events of a later reign, explains in a sentence the fatal defect in the policy of the Mogul Empire. "I desire," he says, "that reflection be made on the unhappy custom of this state, which, leaving the possession of the crown undecided, exposeth it to the conquest of the strongest." At the death of every emperor a struggle took place between the adherents of his various sons, or even grandsons or nephews. The strongest won; and then proceeded to assure a lasting peace by doing away with his rivals. They were either put to death at once, or their eyes were blinded, or they were imprisoned in the hill-fort of Gwalior, or stupefied with opium, or they fled into Persia, or they were forced to make the pilgrimage to Mecca. If the new emperor was not strong or cruel enough to impose the severer punishments, his rivals were sent to govern distant portions of the realm, whence they often returned to vex his power. What may be called the most "prosperous" reigns in India, have been those in which there were the fewest living heirs to the throne. The later Moguls understood this well, and were cruel or crafty enough to carry out the safe policy to its extreme.

In Humayun, we have an example of a Mogul prince whose whole life was spent in agitation or in exile, because he was too affectionate, too filial, and too kind to go to such extremities. His blood was Turki, and not yet Hindu.

Babar, the father of Humayun, fulfilled the highest Turki ideal; he had, as we have seen, "prudence, knowledge, energy, ambition, and generosity — qualities from which nobility draws its name."

A short while before his death, Babar called for his son and heir (Humayun), and charged him that if Allah should grant him the throne and crown, he should not put his brothers to death, but deal kindly with them. Humayun promised obedience, and notwithstanding that his brothers (Kamran, Hindal, Mirza-Askari) were continually opposed to him, and often in open war, he forgot their hostile proceedings as soon as he had vanquished them, for many years, and on many separate occasions.

His kindness was the source of all his woes; and, like many a quality which is amiable in a private person, was well-nigh fatal to the state. It was not until his brothers were removed by war or otherwise, towards the last of his reign, that the Empire had any sort of peace. The Hindus managed such things better; as in the example thus related by an ancient historian:

"In the time of Sultan Mahmud, a Hindu rajah asked his aid against an enemy who aspired to the same sovereignty. He explained the situation to the Sultan thus:

'In my religion the killing of kings is unlawful; but the custom is, that when one king gets another into his power, he makes a small and dark room underneath his own throne, and, having put his enemy into it, he leaves a hole open. Every day he sends a tray of food into that room, until one or the other of the kings dies.'"

Humayun succeeded to the throne in A.D. 1530. His brother Kamran was then governor of Kabul, the capital from whence Babar had set out for his conquest of India. It was clearly Babar's intention that the empire should not be divided, and that Kabul should remain subject to Hindustan. The armies of the emperor were recruited mainly from the Turki, Mogul, and Afghan tribes of this neighborhood, and while there were vast numbers of Hindu auxiliaries, the latter were even less faithful than the Moguls. The officers of the army, especially, had to be drawn from Persia and the countries outside of India. Humayun yielded to Kamran the kingdom of Kabul, and added to it the countries bordering on the Indus, and the Panjab. Prince Hindal was made governor of Sambal, and Mirza-Askari of Mewat. Humayun was emperor of Hindustan, but had not retained the sources of the military power by which alone it could be firmly held. The army still remained, but there were no sure means of increasing, or even of maintaining, its fighting strength.

The emperor's wars began with the invasion of Guzerat and the suppression of rebellions elsewhere. The siege of one of the hill-forts was the occasion of two incidents, each highly characteristic of Humayun. The first stages of the siege had been very unsuccessful. All the practicable approaches to the fort were closely guarded. An almost vertical precipice bounded one side of the plateau on which the fort was built, and Humayun determined to attack it by night on this side. Accordingly steel spikes were prepared and driven right and left, one by one, into the face of the cliff, in the form of a ladder. The emperor himself accompanied a party of three hundred men to the perilous attack, which was successful. Humayun was the forty-first in order to ascend.

It was known that the castle contained much treasure, but a strict search failed to find it. In this juncture Humayun's officers advised that the prisoners be tortured till they confessed. The emperor's counsel was to treat them with kindness, rather, and this was followed. The water was drawn off from a vast cistern, and the treasure found in a chamber beneath it, according to information given by one of the prisoners to his generous captor.

Humayun's great personal bravery and his humanity are well exhibited in these two incidents.

Mirza-Askari, his youngest brother, who was left in charge of these first conquests, soon began to show his want of subordination. At a convivial party he took too much wine, and began to boast that he, too, was "a king and the shadow of Allah." Just at this time the war with Sher-Shah, the Afghan ruler of Berar, began to be serious. The province of Bengal was overrun by Sher-

Shah's forces, and Humayun was committed to a campaign in the rainy season. The soldiers deserted when they could, and Prince Hindal marched off his whole army without permission. Prince Kamran set out with a large force from Kabul, professedly to support the emperor, but in reality to seize the throne if he could do so.

Humayun was forced to retreat towards Agra, and to fight a battle with Sher-Shah in which he was disastrously defeated (A.D. 1539). His queen was captured, and his army totally dispersed. The three brothers met at Agra and were reconciled, and a plan of defence was concerted. It is no part of my intention to recite the events of the next campaign (1540), which ended in the complete success of Sher-Shah (who became emperor of India); in the capture of Delhi and Agra; and in the flight of the emperor and princes to Lahore.

At Lahore another council was held. "It was abundantly manifest to the emperor," says one of the native historians, "that there was no possibility of bringing his brothers and his emirs to any agreement, and he was very despondent."

Prince Hindal marched away in one direction; Prince Kamran "proved faithless," and set off for Kabul. "His brothers then began to shoot the arrows of discord at the target of sovereignty," as the native chronicler has it. Humayun now cast about for a place to set up what remained of his state. Sind, the province just south of Kabul, had been part of Timur's conquests, and whatever Timur had overrun belonged to any of his descendants who could take and keep it; so the emperor set out for Sind with the remnants of his army. On his way he stopped at the camp of Prince Hindal, where he became violently and suddenly enamoured of the young daughter of Hindal's instructor, Sheikh Ali Akbar Jami. She was but fourteen years old, and had been promised in marriage, though not yet betrothed. The emperor decided to marry her at once. Though she was not of suitable rank, her father was a *seiyad*, a descendant of the Prophet Muhammad, and the family was distinguished for learning and piety. The marriage took place the next day.

But Prince Hindal's camp was no place for the head of the state.

"*Ten dervishes can sleep on one rug, but the same climate of the earth cannot contain two kings.*"

Accordingly Humayun plunged into the deserts of Sind, relying on the promises of one of his vassals there, which were not redeemed. During this desert march the party was reduced to the greatest straits, living on berries, lacking water, and harassed by enemies. At the solitary castle of Amerkot, in the midst of the desert, the empress gave birth to her son Akbar (October 15, 1542).

The emperor was encamped some miles distant when the news was brought to him. He had no rich presents to give to the messenger and to his little party, as was customary. He opened a single pod of musk, and distributed the contents among his faithful adherents. The child was named Jalalu-d-din Muhammad Akbar—king of kings—and like the odor of the musk his fame spread throughout the habitable world, according to the loyal wishes of the little band of the emperor's followers.

Kandahar was held by Mirza-Askari as a dependent of Prince Kamran. It was now Humayun's intention to win Askari to his cause, and to find an asylum there. When he was some one hundred and thirty miles from the city, intelligence came that his brother the Mirza was marching against him with hostile intent, and that he must fly for safety. This he did in such haste that the infant Akbar had to be left in the camp with most of the party. Humayun, with the queen and a band of only forty others, fled to Persia. Akbar and those who were left behind were well treated by the Mirza, and removed to Kandahar, and the child was sent to Kabul. As Mirza-Askari and his troops were returning with the young Akbar, one of the emperor's faithful adherents plotted to steal the child from its captors and to return him to his parents. The project was discussed with the guards, and it was decided that Humayun must have had good reasons for leaving his infant son in his brother's hands, and that it would not be right either for the guards to give him up, or for the emperor's immediate followers to interfere with plans not fully understood. Upon this the warrior approached Akbar's litter, and received from the chief in charge of the escort a little fillet, or ribbon, from the child's turban. And with this pledge from one grim warrior to another, he set out to join the fortunes of the flying emperor, and to bring him the last news of the young prince. These are not the savage manners of barbarians.

For three years the emperor had been in Sind, exposed to every hardship. He now set out for Persia to ask the help of Shah Tahmasp, the hereditary friend of his family. His reception was on a grand scale, and all kinds of promises were made on both sides. Humayun agreed to restore Kandahar to Persia, and was obliged to conform to the observances of the *Shia** sect of Muhamma-

* His great ancestor Timur was a *Shia;* though I do not find that this argument was used to change his beliefs.

dans in return for the assistance of a well-equipped army of twelve thousand Persian troops.

On the envelope of the letter which Humayun despatched to the Shah, he wrote these verses:

> *Much hath this aching head endured among the waters,*
> *Much among the rocks and mountains,*
> *And much among the sands of the desert;*
> *But all (these sorrows now) are past.*

Many more sorrows still remained to him, however, before his fortunes were retrieved.

His was a life of constant vicissitude;

> *In the morning he dwelt in a house like Paradise or Heaven,*
> *In the evening he had no longer a dwelling,*
> *As if he had been homeless.*

Prince Kamran was reigning in Kabul. Kandahar had been in his possession; had been captured from him by his brother Prince Hindal; had been recaptured; and was now held by Mirza-Askari. The fourth brother was marching against it at the head of a foreign army. The city was taken after a siege. Askari was pardoned, but he escaped, was recaptured, and imprisoned, and Kandahar was delivered over to the Persians.

As the winter came on, Humayun's troops needed shelter, and as the Persian prince in command opportunely died, the emperor recaptured Kandahar, from the Persians this time, and made it his headquarters. He at once made a winter's march to Kabul. Prince Hindal joined the successful army, and Prince Kamran abandoned his capital and fled; all his forces coming over to the emperor. The young Prince Akbar (now about three years old) was restored to his father. After a few months Humayun set out on an expedition against Badakshan (another one of Timur's conquests); thereupon Kamran returned and again captured Kabul and the young Akbar with it. The forces of Humayun and Hindal immediately returned and closely invested the city. The native writers say: "Kamran, with dastardly feeling, ordered that the prince Akbar should be exposed upon the battlements where the balls and shot of the guns and muskets fell thickest. But Allah Almighty preserved him." Kamran was obliged to fly once more, and Badakshan now fell into *his* hands, but was recaptured by the emperor in 1548. On this occasion Kamran became the prisoner of Humayun and Hindal.

"The emperor displayed the greatest kindness to Kamran, who again received the emblems of sovereignty." Mirza-Askari was set at liberty at this time, and the four brothers ate bread and salt together in sign of amity. In a few months, however, Kamran and Askari again rebelled, and Kabul was again taken by them, and the prince Akbar (a precious hostage) again fell into their hands. Once more the emperor attacked Kabul, and once more Kamran was obliged to fly.

These successive raids, sieges, captures, flights, read like the annals of a band of Sioux. They represent to the life the history of the Moguls before they were permanently established in India. Such "history" is intolerably monotonous and dull, and we are apt to dismiss it with the thought that all this was four centuries ago, among barbarous tribes of Turkistan. But the wars in Europe at the same epoch, were they materially different? We forget that modern war began with Napoleon's campaigns. And as to the barbarous tribes—do we not find almost exact parallels in the cruel revolutions in South American States even to-day? In Chile? In the Argentine? In Brazil? In Honduras? There are no prisoners taken. The corpses of the dead are terribly mutilated. The captured cities are looted, and their inhabitants inhumanly outraged.

It was about this time that Humayun wrote to Kamran to beg him to put an end to their eternal wars. "Oh, my unkind brother," he says, "what are you doing? For every murder that is committed on either side, you will have to answer at the day of judgment. Come and make peace, that mankind may be no more oppressed by our quarrels."

Kamran's answer was the verse:

He who would obtain sovereignty for his bride,
Must woo her across the edge of the sharp sword.

And the wars went on. Breaking into rebellion and ravaging provinces "was an old failing in the family of the Emir Timur," says one of the native historians.

Hindal was sent to capture Kamran, and could have done so, but furthered his escape, and shortly afterwards was himself killed in a battle against the Afghans under Kamran's command. Mirza-Askari was ordered into banishment, and afterwards made the pilgrimage to Mecca, and died (1558) when just beyond Damascus.

It was obvious that no terms could be made with Prince Kamran. He was finally captured, deprived of sight, and he also made the pilgrimage and afterwards died at Mecca, (1557).

Prince Kamran was of a sullen and cruel nature, though bold and enterprising. He inspired no permanent attachment in his officers, or apparently in any one, save his unfortunate wife, who followed him into exile. "You gave me to my husband," said she to her father, "when he was a king and happy, and would take me from him now that he is fallen and blind and miserable; no, I will attend him faithfully wherever he goes."

At the siege of Kabul he murdered the three young children of one of Humayun's officers, and threw their mangled bodies over the walls to the besiegers. He gave the wife of the same nobleman to the rabble in the bazaar to be dishonored. These acts were not only atrocious in themselves, but they were totally contrary to the customs of war.

There is no doubt that the emperor loved him and all his brothers with a sincere affection in spite of treacheries beyond count.

When Kamran presented himself before the throne to make his submission (one of his submissions), he approached humbly with a whip hung around his neck. "Alas! alas!" said the emperor, "there is no need of this; throw it away."

As soon as the ceremony of prostration was over, the emperor exclaimed: "What is past is past. Thus far we have conformed to ceremony. Let us now meet as brothers;"

and embracing him with tears, the emperor made him sit by his side in the place of honor. And then, in a moment, addressing him in Turki (as it were the private speech for two descendants of Timur), he said, "Sit close to me," as if they had been little boys once more.

When Prince Hindal was slain by the Afghans under Kamran, the emperor's camp was on a hill above Hindal's. After the fight was over, Humayun asked for his brother, but "no one had the courage to tell him" that he had been killed. The emperor stood on the little hill in the darkness, and called aloud for Hindal, and sent two different messengers to find him. When he at last learned his brother's fate, he was overwhelmed with grief, and shut himself up in his tent.. One of the high nobles found the emperor in tears, and asked the cause. "Have you not heard of the martyrdom of Mirza Hindal?" The chief had the boldness and good sense to reply: "You lament your own gain; you have one enemy the less"—which was true indeed.

The last rebellion of Prince Kamran, and his atrocious conduct at the siege of Kabul, had made it clear that he deserved no mercy, and that the safety of the state demanded his death. The emperor's councillors were unanimously of this opinion, and they presented a formal written petition and remonstrance, begging that justice be done.

The emperor would not consent, partly from his affection for his turbulent and treacherous brother, partly from memory of his promise to his dying father. Kamran was placed in strict custody, and the next morning orders were given that his eyes should be lanced to deprive him of sight, though not of life. Only so would he be harmless. This was in 1553, after Kamran had been in rebellion more or less constantly for twenty-three years. The emperor's orders were received and executed. Some time afterwards Kamran sent to beg for an interview. "At midnight the emperor, lighted by a lantern, and attended by five or six men of distinction, repaired to Kamran's tent." The emperor sat down and sobbed aloud as the blinded Mirza was led in. He called Allah to witness how little affairs had turned out according to his wishes, and how deeply he felt for his brother's sufferings.

"The Mirza inquired who were in the tent. He was told Mir Tardi Beg, Monaim Beg, Bapus Beg (whose children he had slain), and some others; on which he addressed them and said: 'Be all of you witnesses that whatever has happened to me has proceeded from my own misconduct and fault.' Humayun, much affected, and wishing to put an end to the scene, his voice interrupted by convulsive sorrow, faltered out: 'Let us now repeat the Fateheh.'* The Mirza, upon this, earnestly recommended his children to the emperor's care, who said: 'Set yourself at ease upon that subject; they are my own children.'"

---

* The opening of the Kuran—a prayer. It reads as follows:

Praise be to Allah, the Lord of the Worlds,
The Compassionate, the Merciful,
King of the day of Judgment!
Thee we worship, and Thee we ask for help.
Guide us in the straight way,
The way of those to whom Thou art gracious;
Not of those upon whom is Thy wrath, nor of the erring.

Summarized from Erskine's *Life of Humayun*, Chapter III, Book V.

For the first time in the emperor's reign it was possible for him to undertake operations in the field without fearing the treachery of his own brothers. His previous failures are attributed by (foreign) historians to the levity and weakness of his character. All accounts seem to me to make it clear that, if he had not obeyed his father's admonitions to be kind to his rival brothers, if he had done as his successors did —if he had promptly put them to death—he would have been called a successful ruler; cruel to his brothers, perhaps, but kind to all the world besides. He was often more than kind, even magnanimous and great-hearted.

Saif-Khan had once held his whole army in check for half a day, while his over-lord, Sher-Khan, was making good his escape through a mountain defile. He was finally captured and brought to the emperor, bleeding from three wounds, and expecting death. The emperor said: "Such it behooves a soldier to be; who should lay down his life to advance his master's cause. I set you free; go wherever you choose." Saif answered, "My family is with Sher-Khan; I wish to go to him."

Now, Sher-Khan was a thorn in the side of the Moguls, but Humayun did not hesitate. "I have given you your life; do as you will."

Humayun had a strain of romance in his character, like that of the caliphs who granted favors to poets for their verses, to singers for their songs. "Ask a boon of me."

The following incident, which occurred during the reign of his father, is an excellent example of the romantic impulse and respect for learning which are parts of the Oriental character: A town had been captured, and the soldiers sought everywhere for gold and plunder. "A party of three entered my house," says Maulana Sadu-lla, "and seized my father (who, in studying and teaching the sciences for sixty-five years, had, in the evening of his life, lost his sight) and made him prisoner. Others came and bound me, and sent me as a present to the Mirza (Shah Husain). The Wazir was sitting on a platform when I reached his house, and ordered me to be bound with a chain, one end of which was tied to the platform. I did not grieve for myself, but shed tears for my father's sad condition." The Wazir asked for writing materials, and mended his pen to write, but was called away, leaving no one in the place but the captive.

"I approached the platform, and wrote, on the very paper on which the Wazir intended to write, these verses:

Do not your eyes see how I am weeping,
And do you never say, weep no more?
And does your heart never suggest to you
That you should have pity upon me?"

When the Wazir returned he found the writing, released the poet, robed him in a garment of his own, and introduced him to the Mirza himself, who set the father free, and restored their goods to the two prisoners, dismissing them both with honor.

Everything was now favorable for the reconquest of India. In 1555 the emperor set out from Kabul with fifteen thousand horse, invaded the Panjab, captured Lahore from the Afghans, and took possession of Delhi and Agra. Successful battles, in which the Prince Akbar took part, confirmed him in the possession of Hindustan. He died from the effects of a fall in 1556, half a year after his return to Delhi, and Akbar (then thirteen years old) reigned in his place.

In this last invasion Humayun made a vow that, if Providence restored the sovereignty of India to him, he would never again make slaves of true believers. He was fighting against Afghans, who were Musulmans, and had no scruple in making a pyramid of their heads, in the fashion of Timur the Tartar, but he did not enslave them. This last pyramid of heads was erected seventeen years before the Massacre of Saint Bartholomew.

The success of the first battle for the reconquest of India was splendid; but it produced no change in the equanimity of Humayun's mind. He had always endeavored, he said, to observe three principles of conduct: first of all, integrity of design; then, energy in action; and, finally, moderation in success; ascribing all the glory to an overruling Providence, and nothing to the merits of man.

A very curious chapter might be written

concerning the dreams of the emperors, as recounted in their *Memoirs*. Putting to one side those architecturally elaborate dreams, "I saw an eagle descend from the empyrean and devour a dove, etc.," which are announced by the emperor at his *Durbar*, so that the astrologers may expound them to mean that *he* is the eagle, and his enemy the dove,*—putting these aside, there still remain to us a considerable number of evidently genuine dreams.

We must regard Babar's account of his dream of the flower-gardens as entirely genuine. He recounts it with real pleasure years afterwards. And what a lovely light it throws on his thoughts! In the *Memoirs* of Timur there are several cases of dreams meant to be interpreted in public; but there is one case which seems to me to be entirely real, and to give a glimpse into the monarch's secret mind. He is recounting his "holy war against the infidel Kators" (May, 1398, A.D.). After days of fighting and extreme

* Such, for example, as the dreams of Olympias, mother of Alexander the Great, just before his birth.

fatigue in the mountains, Timur sleeps, and dreams—what? "I dreamed that my sword was bent." When he awakes, this dream, like others, must be expounded. "I interpreted it to be a certain token that Burhan Aghlan had been defeated." As a matter of fact he had been; but it is clear, I think, that the dream itself was true, and not a fabrication intended to convey the idea that Timur was inspired. Here is a small but genuine psychic event. "I dreamed that my sword was bent."

Humayun, too, had dreams *de circonstance* —official dreams, meant to be interpreted in his favor. It is related also that he had a supernatural warning of his death in a dream. He himself says: "I lately rose after midnight to say the stated prayers and retired again to rest; when just before dawn, as I was lying, my eyes shut, but my heart awake, I heard a supernatural voice clearly repeat these verses:

Oh, Lord, of Thine infinite goodness make me Thine own;
Oh, call to Thee thy poor lover; Oh, grant me my release."

He repeated these verses frequently, with

deep emotion; and it was not long afterwards that he met his death by an accident.

Nizamu-d-din-Ahmad was the son of a favorite noble of Babar's and Humayun's court. His history is a standard one, and his estimate of the emperor is at least that of an intelligent observer, who had the fullest opportunity for judgment.* Omitting a few adjectives of convention, there is no reason to doubt that his writing is sincere. He says: "Humayun reigned for more than twenty-five years, and he was fifty-one years of age when he died. His angelic character was adorned with every manly virtue, and in courage he excelled all the princes of the time. All the wealth of Hindustan would not have sufficed to have maintained his generosity. In the sciences of astrology and mathematics he was unrivalled. He made good verses, and all the learned and great and good of the time were admitted to his so-

* He came into high favor with the Emperor Akbar by marching his men twelve hundred miles in twelve days, so as to be present at the celebration of the thirty-fifth anniversary of his coronation at Lahore.

ciety, and passed the night in his company. The light of favor shone on men of ability and worth during his reign. Such was his clemency that he repeatedly pardoned the rebellions of his brother, Mirza Kamran, when he was taken prisoner and was in his power. He was devout and ceremonious in all religious observances."

His "weary indecision" was manifested chiefly in the early part of his reign, and then only in counsel. He was always prompt and brave in action, as became a descendant of Amir Timur. Of Timur we may say what Saint-Simon says of Peter the Great: "Tout montrait en lui la vaste étendue de ses lumières, et *quelque chose de continuellement conséquent.*" All the descendants of Timur were distinguished for personal valor—the courage of the heart. Some of them inherited from their great ancestor that courage of the mind which made him capable of long, patient, unswerving devotion to a resolution once formed. But Humayun was not one of his heirs in this respect. Valor he had, but he was deficient in resolution.

Erskine, the author of a *Life of Humayun*, has given another estimate of his character, which I quote:

"He was a man of great quickness of parts, but volatile, thoughtless, and unsteady. His disposition was naturally generous, friendly, and affectionate; his manners polite, frank, and winning. His generosity finally degenerated into prodigality, his attachments into weakness, and hence to the day of his death he was the prey of flatterers and favorites. He was fond of literature, and delighted in the society of the learned. He was a writer of verses,* and had made, it is said, considerable progress in mathematics and astronomy. At the time of his death he was about to construct an observatory, and had already collected the necessary instruments." "He was a good Musulman, rigid in the observance of the stated prayers and of the ceremonial of the law." "But though he was brave and good-tempered, liberal, and fond of learning, his virtues all bordered on neighboring defects, and produced little fruit."

---

* As was his brother Hindal also.

His father, Babar, has also left us a judgment of him. For a long time Humayun lived at the court and shared in every detail of government, and was the inseparable associate of the emperor, who was never tired of repeating that, as a companion, Humayun had not his equal in the whole habitable world. He was the very flower of humanity and courtesy. His affection for his father was genuine and sincere. In the forty-sixth year of his age he transcribed Babar's *Memoirs* with his own hand, adding a commentary of his own.

He was uniformly kind and considerate to his dependents, devotedly attached to his son Akbar, to his friends, and to his turbulent brothers. The misfortunes of his reign arose, in great part, from his failure to treat them with rigor. But we are obliged to esteem him for this long-suffering consideration, for it was the faithful fulfilment of his promise to his dying father.

The very defects of his character, which render him less admirable as a successful ruler of nations, make us more fond of him as a man. His renown has suffered in that his reign came between the brilliant conquests of Babar and the beneficent statesmanship of 'Akbar; but he was not unworthy to be the son of the one and the father of the other.

CHAPTER IV

SHAH AKBAR THE GREAT, EMPEROR OF HINDUSTAN (A.D. 1556–1605)

THE book of the *Thousand Nights and a Night* begins with these words: "Verily the works and words of those gone before us have become instances and examples to men of our modern day, that folk may view what admonishing chances befel other folk, and may therefrom take warning; and that they may peruse the annals of antique peoples, and all that hath betided them, and be thereby ruled and restrained. Praise therefore be to Allah who hath made the histories of the Past an admonition unto the Present." The works and words of Akbar are worthy to be instances and examples and even admonitions unto the present.

By command of the Emperor Akbar his *wazir*, Abul-fazl, wrote the history of his life,

AKBAR

NUR-MAHAL

SHAH JAHAN

and also a monumental book treating of the government and statistics of the kingdom.*

It is possible from this work to obtain a lively picture of the Empire of the Moguls at the height of its splendor, and the character of its enlightened monarch is set forth in the laws and customs which he prescribed. Abul-fazl's style abounds in smooth flattery, which seems offensive to a Western reader chiefly because it is addressed to a king—and kings are out of date. It is no more fulsome, however, than the address of a candidate for Parliament or Congress to the voters, *his* masters. As reasonable people disregard the latter sort of flattery, so we may also discount the former. I have, therefore, omitted most of the eulogistic passages in Abul-fazl's book, as they are merely conventional, and have but little genuine significance.

---

* This volume, the *Ain-i-Akbari*, has been twice translated: by Francis Gladwin (1800) and by Professor Blochmann (1873). The edition of 1873 is supplemented by a series of notes, so elaborate, so interesting, so learned, as to give the work of Abul-fazl a double title to be regarded as one of the world's great books. I have quoted from both translations in this chapter.

Akbar was the son of Humayun, and came to the throne in 1556. He died in 1605, after a reign of nearly fifty years. The history of his wars and conquests is far less interesting than the picture of his civil government.

Abul-fazl's book enables us to trace the finger of the monarch in every detail of the administration of a vast and well-ordered empire which extended from Persia to the Ganges, and from Cashmere to the Deccan. A glance at the table of contents gives the following chapter-headings among many: The Household; the Royal Treasuries; the Jewel Office; the Mint; the Harem; the Equipage for Journeys; Regulations for the Encampment of the Army; Ensigns of Royalty; Perfume Office; Painting Gallery; Artillery; Stables for Elephants, Horses, Camels, Oxen; Regulations for the Public Fights of Animals; Regulations for Teaching in the Public Schools; Revenue Department; Particular Account of Each One of the Fifteen Provinces Governed by Viceroys; Rent-roll of the Empire; Religious Toleration; Description of Hindustan—its Inhabitants—its Doctrines—its Customs, etc., etc., etc., and a thousand things besides.

"It is universally agreed," says Abul-fazl, "that the noblest employments are the reformation of the manners of the people, the advancement of agriculture, the regulation of the offices, and the discipline of the army; and these desirable ends are not to be attained without studying to please the people, joined with good management of the finances and exact economy in the expenses of the state; but when these are kept in view, *every class of people enjoys prosperity*."

What an immense change of ideal this paragraph denotes from that of Timur, Akbar's ancestor! The prosperity of the people! Compare this with the terrible marches and sieges of Timur, each marked with its pyramids of human heads. The advance of agriculture! This is the ideal of the descendant of those Turki warriors who jeered at wheat, calling it "the top of a weed."

The emperor appointed treasurers for

each department, who kept daily, monthly, quarterly, and yearly accounts. Diamonds and other jewels belonging to the crown were valued and classed; pearls were strung in scores, and at the end of each string the seal was affixed, that they might not be unsorted or stolen. Each ruby of price bore the inscription, "The magnificent ruby." These jewels cannot all be lost. Are any of Akbar's rubies in European collections to-day? A mint with fixed regulations and with paid officials was established, and rules for the fineness of the precious metals were laid down.* Light coins were received according to established discounts. "Every money matter will be satisfactorily settled, when the parties express their minds clearly,

* Among his jewellers was an Englishman, Mr. William Leades. The king "entertained him very well, gave him a house and five slaves, a horse, and every day six shillings in money." Leades' history is curious. He was one of four Englishmen who travelled from Syria and Persia to India in 1583, bearing letters from Queen Elizabeth to the Great Mogul. After many adventures they came to very different ends. One of the company (Storey) became a monk at Goa; Leades entered Akbar's service; Newberry died on the journey home; and Fitch returned to England in 1591, and published an account of his voyages.

then take a pen, and write down the statement in legible handwriting." As we read these paragraphs we do not seem to be in the middle ages, until, by accident, we see that "metals are formed of vapor and exhalation, which is to be particularly learned from books of natural philosophy." Akbar brought his coins to a fixed standard of purity and improved their shape. They were weighed against standard agate weights. One of them bore for a legend:

> *The best coin is that which is employed in supplying men with the necessaries of life, and which benefits the companions in the road of God.*

Special coinage alloys were invented by Akbar himself, who experimented in all departments from religion to metallurgy. Minute rules prescribed how the betting on deer-fights should be conducted; and "the leanness of elephants was divided into thirteen classes,"—to see if their food had been stolen.

Akbar inherited his desire for classifying and organizing everything from his father

Humayun, in whom the systematic tendency was strongly developed, but whose vagabond life did not permit him to carry out his tendencies to the full. Humayun in the beginning of his reign divided all his people into three classes. The royal family, the nobles, the military chiefs, were the first class; the religious hermits, the descendants of the Prophet, the *literati*, the law officers, the astronomers, and the poets, "besides other great and respectable men," were the second class; while those who were young and lovely, the singers and musicians, were the third. The occupations of the days of the week were apportioned to these three classes, two days to each class, etc. The more serious occupation of guarding his kingship, and even his life, soon broke up this artificial and rather silly scheme, of which I have given but a very small part.

Abul-fazl writes thus (feelingly) of the Harem, or Seraglio: "There is, in general, great inconvenience arising from a number of women; but his majesty, out of the abundance of his wisdom and prudence, has made it subservient to public advantage; for by contracting marriages with the daughters of the princes of Hindustan and of other countries, he secures himself against insurrections at home, and forms powerful alliances abroad.* The harem is an enclosure of such immense extent as to contain a separate room for each one of the women, whose number exceeds five thousand. They are divided into companies, and a proper employment is assigned to each individual. Over each of these companies a woman is appointed to rule. And one is selected for the care of the whole, in order that the affairs of the harem may be conducted with the same regularity as the other departments of the state."

The harem was thus a state bureau; its chief was Maham Anka, who had been Akbar's nurse and faithful attendant during the perilous adventures of his childhood, and who was,

* It is often said that one of Akbar's wives was a Christian princess. It is worth while to give this foot-note to a correction of the error. Of all the royal families of the proud *Rajputs*, one only, that of Oudipur, steadily rejected all marriages with the house of the Mogul conquerors, and to this day has kept its blood pure, according to the ancient Rajput customs.

in fact, his prime minister in the early years of his reign.

"Each one receives a salary equal to her merit. The pen cannot measure the extent of the emperor's largesses; but here shall be given some account of the *monthly* stipend of each. The ladies of the first quality receive from 1,610 rupees * down to 1,028 rupees. Some of the principal servants have from fifty-one down to twenty rupees, and others are paid from two rupees up to forty." "Whenever any of this multitude of women want anything, they apply to the treasurer." "The inside of the harem is guarded by women," and there were eunuchs, porters, and military guards at different distances outside, each in a prescribed position.

The equipages for journeys and encampments were as complex as a town. For it must be remembered that when the emperor moved from a city, the inhabitants moved with him; merchants, families, servants, and slaves. The camp was simply the city under tents.

* A rupee may be taken as about fifty-five cents in Akbar's time.

Akbar had various seals. One bore his name alone; another, the name of all of his ancestors up to Timur; for petitions a seal was used with the inscription:

> *Rectitude is the means of pleasing God.*
> *I never saw any one lost in the straight road.*

"His majesty even extends his attentions to the kitchen department, and has made many wise regulations concerning it. He eats but once in the course of twenty-four hours, and he always leaves off with an appetite. But what is required for the harem is going on from morning to night." "Trusty people are appointed to the kitchen department, and his majesty is not unwatchful of their conduct." In Babar's time an awning was spread over the kitchen to insure that poison should not be dropped from above, and all the cooking was done under guard. Moreover, attempts against the emperor's life were provided against by the appointment of *tasters*, and unmindful tasters were flayed alive! The same precautions were taken by Akbar, and the dishes were sent from the kitchen in napkins whose corners were fastened by a seal. "The copper utensils for his majesty's use are tinned twice a month; those for the princes and the harem only once in that time." Everything was regulated in this kingdom of ordinances. Akbar drank only the waters of the Ganges, cooled with saltpetre. "Saltpetre, which in the composition of gun-powder supplies heat, has been discovered by his majesty to be also productive of cold." *

All the water for Akbar's use and all the provisions were kept in vessels under seal, and the magazines and gardens were guarded by trusty servants. This was necessary in a realm where treachery abounded, the classic land of poisons.

The receipts for thirty dishes are given by the *wazir*. I shall only quote one, for the benefit of young housekeepers. "CHICKEE.

---

* The philosophy of Abul-fazl is like that of the little girl in *Punch*, who gazes at a tortoise, and remarks how passing strange it is that the animal which supplies her with her combs should possess so extremely little hair.

Ibn Batuta tells us that there was a special seal-bearer under Sultan Mahmud (A.D. 997–1030) whose duty it was to seal the water-jars used by that emperor.

Ten pounds of wheat flour made into a paste and washed until it is reduced into two pounds; one pound of clarified butter, and the same quantity of onions; saffron, cardamoms, and cloves, each quarter of an ounce; cinnamon, round pepper, and coriander seed, each half an ounce; green ginger and salt, each an ounce and a half. *Some add lemon juice.*"

To the Western palate it seems indifferent whether the lemon were added or not. A hundred dishes was the usual *menu* for Akbar's dinner. "One day when his majesty was at dinner, it occurred to his mind that probably the eyes of some hungry one had fallen upon the food. How, therefore, could he eat it while the hungry were debarred from it? He therefore gave orders that every day some hungry persons should be fed with some of the food prepared for himself, and that afterwards he should be fed." "His majesty has a great disinclination for flesh, and he frequently says, 'Providence has provided variety of food for man, but through gluttony and ignorance he destroys living creatures and makes his body a tomb for beasts. If I were not a king I would leave off eating flesh at once, and now it is my intention to quit it by degrees.'" And in fact he always abstained from meat on two days in every week. Akbar was exceedingly fond of fruit, and introduced many varieties from Persia and Tartary. The best muskmelons came from Tartary, and cost two and a half rupees each; apples from Samarkand were ten for a rupee.

"His majesty is exceedingly fond of perfumes, and the presence-chamber. is constantly scented with flowers, and fumigated with perfumes burned in gold and silver censers." His faithful minister gives many receipts for compounding scents. A long list is also given of the flowers of the country and of their seasons for blossoming.

"*Of Marriages:* His majesty does not approve of every one marrying more than one wife. He censures old women who take young husbands. His majesty maintains that *the consent of the bride and bridegroom,* and the permission of the parents, *are absolutely necessary.*" This is almost inconceivably advanced doctrine, when we remember the time and place. A consideration of the juvenile marriages of the Hindus had formed Akbar's opinions on this point.

"Every day some capable person reads to his majesty, who hears every book from beginning to end. He always marks with the date of the month the place where he leaves off. There is hardly a work of science, of genius, or of history, but has been read to his majesty, and he is not tired of hearing them repeated, but always listens with great avidity." Many books were translated by his command, and a history of all parts of the world for the last thousand years was prepared by his order. Akbar applied to the Pope of Rome for a copy of the Pentateuch, having already in his possession, so he says, the Evangelists and the Psalms in Persian.*

"All civilized nations have schools; but Hindustan is particularly famous for its seminaries." As in everything else in the empire, Akbar had improvements to suggest; and

* One of the Persian poets declares that the Psalms were originally written by David in the Persian dialect! (Ross's Saadi.)

"what used to take up years, is now accomplished in a few months, to the astonishment of every one." "Every boy should read books on morals, arithmetic, agriculture, mensuration, geometry, astronomy, physiognomy, household matters, the rules of government, (theological, mathematical, and physical) sciences, and history—all of which may be gradually acquired."

"His majesty takes great delight in the painting-gallery, and having patronized this art from the beginning of his reign, has caused it to arrive at high perfection." Every week pictures were submitted to him and the artists rewarded. A list of the eighteen most eminent painters of his court is given. Books were illuminated also, and one (in twelve volumes) had no less than fourteen hundred illustrations. Portraits of all the chief officers were made, and bound in a volume "wherein the past are kept in lively remembrance, and the present are insured immortality."

The library of his poet-laureate (the brother of Abul-fazl) contained forty-six hundred manuscripts, and Akbar's was far more complete. In Jahangir's time, the walls of the palace at Lahore were literally covered with portraits and other pictures. Timur's picture gallery at Samarkand contained mural paintings of his battles in Hindustan. "There are many that hate painting," says Akbar, "but such men I dislike. It appears to me as if a painter had quite peculiar means of recognizing God. For a painter in sketching anything that has life, and in devising its limbs, one after the other, must come to feel that he cannot bestow individuality upon his work, and is thus forced to think of God, the giver of life."

In the year 1570 Akbar laid the foundations of his city Futtehpore-Sikri, near the residence of the Saint Selim Ṣhisti, after whom his eldest son was named (Prince Selim, afterwards Jahangir). The site was not really suitable, and the city was abandoned in 1584. Its ruins are to-day a wonder to travellers. The great fort at Agra was built by him also If he had not been succeeded by two kings with a passion for architecture, like Jahangir, and especially Shah Jahan, Akbar would have been famous as a builder also. There is a sober solidity to many of his constructions which renders them to-day at once imposing and characteristic.

Particular rules were laid down for the manufacture of artillery and of small arms; and all these pieces were tested by Akbar himself. It appears that with one single musket the emperor had killed nineteen hundred separate beasts—for in his hunting, as in everything else, he kept precise accounts. Each one of the emperor's private guns had its appropriate name.

Abul-fazl's description of the elephants of India is most interesting, but it is far too long for quotation. It may be remarked that he says that the natural life of this beast, "like that of man," is one hundred and twenty years. It is noteworthy, too, that before Akbar's time it was considered unlucky to allow tame elephants to breed; "but his majesty has surmounted this prejudice"—this superstition.

"His majesty being very fond of horses, droves are constantly arriving, so that at this day there are in his stables twelve thousand horses." Akbar paid a salary to an official of his stables, whose business it was to burn a kind of mustard-seed to avert the evil eye. The express-service of the empire was done on swift camels, and not by horses. At every six miles on the principal routes a postman was stationed, and besides these "a great number of camel-riders are waiting in the palace for the purpose of carrying orders or messages, the instant they are ready to be despatched, to the most distant extent of the realm."

"Whenever his majesty marches at the head of his army the road is carefully measured, by means of bamboo rods, by persons appointed for that purpose. The units of measure were one *guz* (equal to about thirty-three inches), and one *crouh*, which equals five thousand *guz*." The ancient definitions of these standard measures are worth quoting, that we may comprehend the necessity for some of the reforms of Akbar. In one province the *crouh,* or standard measure, was "the greatest distance at which may be heard the ordinary lowing of an ox." In another, "a man is to pluck a green leaf, and, placing it upon his head, to walk with it until it becomes dry; this distance, they say, is a *crouh.*" I quote part of one of the tables given:

" 6 hairs of a mule's tail . . .	*make*	one barleycorn.
6 barley corns	"	one inch.
24 inches	"	one *guz.*"

The "barleycorn" of our old arithmetics makes its appearance here.

"His majesty is exceedingly fond of music, and has a perfect knowledge of its principles. This art, which the generality of people use as the means of inducing sleep, serves to amuse him, and to keep him awake."

The Emperor Babar was not fond of Hindus, nor of Hindustan, as we have seen; but Abul-fazl says:

"Summarily the Hindus are religious, affable, courteous to strangers, cheerful, enamored of knowledge, lovers of justice, given to retirement, able in business, grateful, admirers of truth, and of unbounded fidelity in all their dealings. Their soldiers know not what it is to fly from the field of battle. They have great respect for their teachers, and make no account of their lives when they can devote them to the service of God." This unbounded panegyric ought to stand alone. Unfortunately, in another place, Abul-fazl expresses a different opinion; he says: "In short, some have the disposition of angels, and others are demons. There are some who for the merest trifle will commit the greatest outrages."

As Abul-fazl's work was to pass under the eye of the king, he improved the opportunity to give little moral lessons to inculcate an even temper, or to strengthen the position of good *wazirs*. There are many such passages, of which I shall quote but one:

"A wise prince never suffers himself to be led away by reports, but exercises his circumspection and makes diligent investigation, seeing that truth is scarce and falsehood common; and it behoveth him to be more especially doubtful of whatever is said to the prejudice of those whom he has distinguished by peculiar marks of his favor, as the world in general bears them enmity even without cause, and the wicked frequently put on the appearance of virtue to compass the destruction of the innocent." But Akbar, though hasty in his temper, was faithful to his friends; and his *wazir*, in particular, enjoyed his favor to his last day, and was sincerely mourned after his death.

"*The Manner in which His Majesty spends His Time.*

"On this depends the welfare and happiness of all ranks of people. It is his majesty's constant endeavor to gain and secure the hearts of all men. Amidst a thousand cares, he suffers not his temper to be disturbed, but is always cheerful. He is ever striving to do that which is most acceptable to the Deity, and employs his mind on profound and abstract speculations. He listens to what every one has to say. He never suffers himself to be led away by wrath. Others employ story-tellers to lull them to sleep, but his majesty, on the contrary, listens to them to keep himself awake. He exercises upon himself both inward and outward austerities, and pays regard to external forms, in order to avoid cause for reproach. He never laughs at or ridicules any religion or sect; * he never omits the performance of any duty. He is continually returning thanks unto Providence and scrutinizing his own conduct. He is ever sparing of the lives of offenders, wishing to bestow happiness upon all his subjects. His majesty is visible to everybody twice in the course of twenty-four hours. He often appears at an open window, and from thence receives petitions *without the intervention of any person*. He considers an equal distribution of justice and the happiness of his subjects as essential to his own felicity."

Making every allowance for the obsequiousness and servility of an Oriental official, it is clear that Abul-fazl is here describing something between the ideal which Akbar really set before himself, and the reality which he

* This is by no means true, as the present chapter will abundantly show.

attained. The ideal was nearly the highest possible. Perhaps no ruler but Marcus Aurelius has had a higher one. The reality must be judged by the practical success of his plans. I do not know that many Western rulers have surpassed him, and certainly no Oriental monarch has come near to this excellence.*

What, then, in fact, should a benevolent and wise ruler do for his subjects? The *acts* of Akbar's government might almost be taken for a model of practice, just as Timur's Institutes are admirable theory. He surveyed the

---

* Sher-Shah, the Afghan king who drove Humayun from Hindustan, and whose dynasty was in its turn overthrown by Akbar, seems to have originated very many of the administrative reforms which are usually credited to Akbar; but he was far behind him in religious toleration. Akbar was fortunate in having a great minister of finance, Rajah Todar Mal, who had learned his business under Sher-Shah. Abul-fazl says of him, that "for honesty, rectitude, manliness, knowledge of business, and administrative skill, he was without a rival." Two of Akbar's advisers, then, were men of the very highest ability, and one of them, Abul-fazl, a wonderfully liberal and elevated statesman. Mr. Horace Hayman Wilson, in Mill's *India*, declares explicitly: "Whatever merit there may have been in the financial arrangements of Akbar, it belonged to the Hindus"—that is, essentially to Rajah Todar Mal. It required a great king to utilize such ministers.

land and divided it into classes. He equalized the taxes. In times of famine and distress he partly or totally remitted them. "His majesty abolished all arbitrary taxes. He fixed standard measures; after which he ascertained the value of the lands, and fixed the revenue accordingly." The duties on manufactures were reduced one-half (to five per cent.). The complicated and unjust systems of official fees were either totally abolished or much simplified, and the officials were usually paid by the state, instead of extorting for themselves what the peasants could give and yet exist. Full statistics were collected, and the imposts were then fixed for a period of ten years. In a thousand ways the affairs of the state were settled on a definite basis of law, instead of on shifting caprice. There is no space to present the details of these enactments. Perhaps the quickest method of exhibiting them will be to give brief extracts from the "instructions for the officers." These were the actual rules by which the empire was administered, at least during the

The Viceroy.—"He must constantly keep in view the happiness of the people; he shall not take away life until after the most mature deliberation; those who apply for justice, let them not be afflicted with delay; let him accept the excuse of the penitent; let the roads be made safe; let him consider it his duty to befriend the industrious husbandman."

The Cazi (judge).—"Divesting himself of partiality and avarice, let him distinguish the oppressor from the oppressed, and act accordingly."

The Cootwal (a kind of provost-marshal).—"His own conduct must be upright and strictly honest; the idle he shall oblige to learn some trade; upon coins short of weight he shall take exactly the deficiency (and no more); he shall prohibit the drinking of spirituous liquors, but need not take pains to discover what men do in secret; he shall not allow a widow to be burned contrary to her inclinations."

The Collector of the Revenues.—"He must consider himself the immediate friend of the husbandman; he must not require any intermediary; he must assist the needy husbandman with loans of money, and receive payment at distant and convenient periods; he must reward skilful management; let him see that his demands do not exceed his agreements; let him collect the revenue with kindness; vexatious taxes must not be exacted."

These extracts are but specimens of the formal and elaborate instructions given to the officials. The originals of some of these documents exist to-day. There is reason to believe that they were obeyed in a great degree. At all events, they certainly represent the ideal towards which this monarch strove.

His life covered the years A.D. 1542–1605. Cæsar Borgia was but just dead. The horrors of the sack of Rome had endured for seven months of the year 1527. Elizabeth of England reigned from 1558 to 1603. The very first English book of any scientific value (Robert Recorde's Arithmetic) was printed in 1540. The Massacre of St. Bartholomew was in 1572. The Spanish Armada was defeated in 1588.

Shakespeare's first poem was printed in 1593. Jordano Bruno was burned in Rome in 1600. The first treatise on the law of nations, and the Habeas Corpus Act were nearly a century later. Witches were executed in England until 1712, and were burned in France till 1718; in Spain, till 1780. Luther (*circa* 1530) had personal encounters with the devil. When Blaise Pascal was a year old he was bewitched, and only rescued by the application of a plaster made from herbs plucked before sunrise, by a virgin of seven years, and bruised down with the blood of a cat belonging to the sorceress (1621). Kepler's aunt was burned as a witch, and he had the greatest difficulty in saving his mother from the same fate (1620); Kepler himself, the leading man of science in central Europe, declared that the reality of witchcraft could not be denied. He died in 1630. Russia, France, Spain, Italy, Germany, were no better governed than India. It might very well be debated if the actual condition of the English people was to be preferred to that of the Hindus of the central provinces under the comparatively mild rule of Akbar.*

Akbar was but little over thirteen years of age when he ascended the throne. From this time until he was eighteen, he remained under the tutelage of a great noble, Bairam Khan, his prime minister and guardian. From him Akbar learned the art of war; and he saw in daily operation the rough and ready methods of government which were usual. We might call them the methods of Timur. They were, in fact, Timur's methods modified by the progress of culture and chivalry under intelligent and generous princes

* It is difficult for us to realize the veritable condition of the peasantry of Europe in the beginning of the seventeenth century. If it should seem that the comparison in the text is too favorable to India, I beg to refer to a graphic portrayal of the wretchedness of the peasants of France a century after Akbar, in the *Mémoires de Saint-Simon*, year 1709, chapter xxix. The misery of 1709 in France was exceptional, no doubt. But Akbar's policy provided for exceptional cases by distributing food, remitting taxes, and loaning money. In this connection reference may also be made to Feillet, *Histoire du Paupérisme*, and to La Bruyère's famous paragraph on the French peasants, in his chapter *De l'Homme*. The facts for England are to be found in Professor Thorold Rogers' *History of Prices*, and some conclusions therefrom in the *Nineteenth Century* for June, 1893, page 932.

like Babar and Humayun. There is little doubt that Akbar's reflections on these methods impressed upon him at least one grave defect. If he were to rule in India, it was essential to be at peace with the great Hindu chiefs.* This could not be unless the old political methods were made more liberal. Moreover, the fundamental law of every Muhammadan empire was the law of the Kuran, interpreted, be it remembered, by bigots.

It was clear that the millions of Hindus could not be ruled by such a code. Political and religious toleration were therefore forced upon Akbar, and he became convinced that the old methods must be greatly changed. It is probable that Bairam Khan did not share these views; it is, at any rate, certain, that the harem intrigued against him. In his eighteenth year Akbar dismissed Bairam (sending him on the pilgrimage to Mecca, pardoning his outbreak into rebellion, and treating him with considerate generosity), and

* There were nearly a hundred Hindu princes, many of them very powerful.

assumed the sole authority. From this year (1560) Akbar ruled alone. Until the eighteenth year of his reign (1573) he was perpetually occupied in suppressing rebellion, or in conquering new provinces; and it was not until then that his vast possessions were reduced to an orderly empire. These early years were necessarily years of strife and of successful military activity.

Abul-fazl came to his court in 1574, at the end of this first period. Up to this time Akbar had been a good Muslim, making pilgrimages, and circumambulating the tombs of saints. This second period of his reign (1574–1605), though not free from wars and rebellions, is chiefly memorable for its peaceful triumphs.

"His majesty, who knows what high regard is due to approved customs of antiquity, is continually endeavoring to make himself acquainted with them; and then, regardless of who was the institutor, he adopts such as appear proper."

Toleration of the Hindu and Persian heretics was, particularly in the latter part of his reign, the keynote of Akbar's political conduct. As Abul-fazl well says, "Religious persecution, after all, defeats its own ends; it obliges men to conceal their opinions, but produces no change in them." In the flowery language of the *Thousand and One Nights*, this principle deserves to be "written with needle-gravers on the corners of the eye-balls, as a warner to whoso will be warned."

His early toleration in religious matters was succeeded by the establishment of an eclectic religion in which Akbar himself represented Deity much as the Roman emperors had done. The sun, as the symbol of celestial power, was worshipped daily by the ruler, while the people saluted the emperor as the representative of that power on earth. Abul-fazl has various references to "The Divine Faith," or the "Divine Monotheism," as the new belief was called, and I purpose to extract a few of them.

There is nothing more curious in human history than the formation of a creed. It must not rudely reject all the beliefs of the past, but it may modify them so as to meet the demands of the present. "The Divine Faith" was prosperous under Akbar, and it survived for a while under his immediate successor, but it died a natural death as time went on; and India was left under the sway of its manifold native sects and of little-altered Islamism.

Four times daily the emperor returned thanks to the Deity—at daybreak, at noon, at sunset, and at midnight. "All these grand mysteries are in honor of God; and if ignorant people cannot comprehend their meaning, who is to be blamed? Every one is sensible that it is our duty to praise our benefactor, and consequently to praise this Fountain of Light, the Sun, and more especially behoveth it princes so to do, seeing that this sovereign of the heavens sheddeth his divine influence upon the monarchs of the earth. His majesty has also great veneration for fire in general, and for lamps, since they are to be accounted rays of the greater light." Once a year, near the vernal equinox, fire was brought down from heaven by a crystal lens, and "this celestial fire was committed to the care of proper persons" (Abul-fazl himself being the chief of these); "and when the year expires they catch new fire." Huge candles of camphor, in candlesticks of massy gold and silver, lighted the emperor's camp by night. So minutely were his affairs regulated, that the number of *flambeaux* in the palace (fire-pots of torches) was regulated by the age of the moon. At new moon eight *flambeaux* were lighted; from the fourth to the tenth day, one less was burned each night, so that on the tenth day one was sufficient, and so on throughout the lunation. The very quantity of oil and rags per torch was specified.

Again he says, *Of Spiritual Guidance*, that "by the decrees of God mankind are in general disposed to applaud their own actions, and to condemn those of others;" "thus different bodies of men hold different beliefs, and amuse themselves with their respective dreams and illusions." "Sometimes, through the good fortune of mankind, the truth may be revealed. When a private person arrives at such a degree of knowledge, he keeps silence from the dread of savage beasts in human forms; but if this light is given to an emperor, as the astrologers knew that it was given to Akbar," then, indeed, is fit occasion to speak. "His majesty did, however, for some time, cast a veil over this mystery, that it might not be known to strangers."

Finally he proclaimed his divine attributes, and his miraculous power was manifested in various ways; those who came near him increased in knowledge, and the poor and needy loved him. He foretold the future and cured diseases. "His majesty instructs others as circumstances may require; and many, according to their capacities, are recreated with sublime discourses." But, says the courtier, "this is not the proper place for giving a full account of the manner in which he instructs mankind, nor of the numerous miracles he has performed. Should my life be sufficiently prolonged, and should I have leisure enough, it is my intention to compose a volume on this interesting subject."

It is plain that the good Abul-fazl was willing to postpone his promised volume, and it is clear enough that "the Divine Faith" had no real interior vitality. This religion was too much based on reasonings. There were no mighty miracles and signs manifest upon which to rest it. The "miracles" ascribed to Akbar are poor and cheap affairs. "Faith is believing what is not true," as the little school-child wrote. Akbar did not make sufficient demands on the credulity of his sectaries. They acquiesced in his lordship; they rejoiced in the sunshine of his favor; they prospered under his just and even rule. The state religion endured under him, and under his immediate successor; but even the emperors held it lightly, and admitted Jesuits and Mollahs to open debates in their presence, and proposed to put the power of prayer to physical tests.

Akbar's toleration is well summed up in an inscription written by Abul-fazl for one of the temples of Cashmere:

Oh God, in every temple I see people that see Thee, and in every language I hear spoken, people praise Thee.

Polytheism and Islam feel after Thee.
Each religion says, Thou art One, without equal.
If it be a mosque, people murmur the holy prayer; and if it be a Christian church, people ring the bell from love to Thee.
Sometimes I frequent the Christian cloister, and sometimes the mosque,
But it is Thou whom I seek from temple to temple.
Thy elect have no dealings with heresy nor with orthodoxy; for neither of these stands behind the screen of Thy truth.
Heresy to the heretic, and religion to the orthodox,
But the dust of the rose-petal belongs to the heart of the perfume-seller.

The foregoing account is mostly drawn from Abul-fazl's book of the *Regulations of Akbar.* I have not been willing to interrupt its orderly flow with commentaries from the other native historians of the reign, but have preferred to present extracts from their various accounts together in one place.

The Emperor Jahangir gives us this portrait of Akbar, his father, in his *Memoirs.* It would seem to be of the highest authority. He says: "My father used to hold discourse with learned men of all persuasions; though he was illiterate, yet, from constantly conversing with learned and clever persons, his language was so polished that no one could discover from his conversation that he was entirely uneducated. He understood the elegancies of poetry and prose so well, that it is impossible to conceive of any one more proficient." I had read this description a great many times, and failed to reconcile entire illiteracy with the possession of delicate critical faculties, when I found what I suppose to be a solution. Akbar ascended the throne at the age of thirteen, after a youth full of accidents and perils and vicissitudes. From a paragraph in the history of Mir Yahya Masum, whose son was chosen to be his preceptor in the second year of his reign, it appears that "at that time the prince knew not how to read and write." The very phrase "at that time" indicates that he subsequently became "literate." And Jahàngir's description probably means no more than that his father was not educated in his youth, which is not surprising, considering the events of the last years of Humayun's troubled reign. This instructor of Akbar's—Mir Abdullatif—was the first to teach him the principle of "*peace-with-all,*" a doctrine which was then definite enough to have a special name. In Akbar's sixteenth year he had another tutor, and read with him "poems in mystic language."

A highly educated youth in those days would read and write Arabic, understand its grammar and its rules of poetic composition. Large portions of the Kuran he would know by heart. Persian would be his mother-tongue, and he would be able to repeat nearly the whole of the poems of Hafiz and Saadi, and many verses from Firdausi. He would be familiar with the biographies of kings and princes. He would know a little mathematics and astronomy and somewhat of music. The descendants of Timur kept up a knowledge of the Turki language certainly as late as the time of Jahangir, who could compose in Turki.*

"Akbar was of middling stature, but with a tendency to be tall; wheat-color complexion, rather dark than fair; black eyes and eye-

---

* For an amusing sketch of a perfect education, the reader should refer to the tale of Abu-al-Husn and his slave-girl Tawaddud in Lady Burton's *Arabian Nights*, vol. iii., p. 277.

brows ; stout body ; open forehead and chest ; long arms and hands. . . . He had a very loud voice, and a very elegant and pleasant way of speech. His manners and habits were quite different from those of other persons, and his visage was full of godly dignity,"—so says his son Jahangir.

Like his ancestors, Akbar was an eager hunter. In one day he personally slew sixteen of the swift wild asses of the desert. He ornamented the mile-posts near Agra with "some hundreds of thousands of the horns of stags" which had been killed in his hunts. He once rode two hundred and twenty miles within forty-eight hours. "His history is filled with instances of romantic courage, and he seems to have been stimulated by an instinctive love of danger as often as by any rational motive." He perfectly fulfilled the ideals of personal chivalry which were current in his day. These ideals had their sources among the Arabs, and in India they were modified by the Rajput standards of military valor—no mean origin and descent. The following instances of chivalry and loyalty show how fully these ideals were carried out in practice by the Turki warriors. One of Timur's sons (Jahangir) was pursuing Kummer Addyn and overtook him. A soldier threw himself forward and in a tone of authority cried out, "*I* am Kummer Addyn," —and perished in his master's stead.

Qasim Kokah and Babar were taken prisoners by an Uzbeg Khan. Qasim announced that *he* was Babar, and was cut to pieces, leaving Babar to escape. Bairam Khan, a high officer of Humayun's (and the guardian of young Akbar), was surprised by an enemy. Abul Qasim, a man of imposing stature, was mistaken for Bairam, and was about to be killed, when the latter stepped forward and said in a manly voice, "I am Bairam." "No," said Abul Qasim, "he is only my attendant; and, brave and faithful as he is, he wishes to sacrifice himself for me. So let him off." It was so. Abul was slain, and his over-lord Bairam escaped.

Akbar captured the strong castle of Chitor after a heroic defence by Rajah Jeimall (whom Akbar shot with his favorite gun named *Sangram*) and his brother. To honor the extraordinary valor of these high-born adversaries, Akbar set up their statues, mounted on elephants, at the gates of his royal city of Delhi. Says Bernier, "These two huge elephants, mounted by the two heroes, are full of grandeur, and fill me with indescribable awe and respect."

One more instance must suffice. To suppress a dangerous revolt, Akbar marched an army of three thousand men four hundred and fifty miles in nine days, in the rainy season, and completely surprised the rebel army (which was much larger than his own) sleeping in their tents. The few who were alert could not believe that they saw the emperor, since there were no war elephants in his train. "The feeling ran through the royal ranks that it was unmanly to fall upon an enemy unawares, and that they would wait until he was roused." Akbar accordingly ordered the trumpeters to sound the onset; the rebel army prepared for action, and was routed and overwhelmed.

While Jahangir, the son of Akbar, was

yet the heir-apparent, his tendency to cruel punishments had begun to show itself. In all matters of state he was ever inexorable and relentless. On one occasion he ordered a servant, who had joined a conspiracy against his life, to be flayed alive. When this came to the ears of his father, whose policy in such cases was usually so very different, and whose nature was kind, he wrote his son a severe letter, reprobating his conduct, and saying that as he himself was unable to see even a sheep stripped of its skin without horror, it was inconceivable to him how his son could inflict such an awful punishment upon a fellow creature. Akbar could be very brief and peremptory, however, upon occasion. To a dilatory envoy he sent this letter: "If thou dost not return to court with Asad, thou shalt see what will happen to thee and to thy children." Various anecdotes show that he had a violent, though not a vindictive, temper.*. His clemency was of very gradual growth.

* See Herbert's *Travels*, edition of 1638, p. 71.

"The emperor used to retire after evening prayers, during which time the servants dispersed, assembling again when they expected his majesty to reappear. That evening he happened to come out earlier than usual. He saw a luckless lamplighter coiled up in a careless sleep. Enraged at the sight, he ordered him to be thrown from the tower, and he was dashed into a thousand pieces." The officers on guard were disgraced and their places given to others. We have this story from one of the latter. In the twelfth year of his reign eight thousand Rajputs were slaughtered after the surrender at Chitor; in the seventeenth he ordered the tongue of a captive to be cut out; in the eighteenth he raised a pyramid of two thousand heads in the fashion of Timur; and in various portions of his earlier reign he sanctioned, or directly ordered, barbarous punishments and torture. This was before he had come under the influence of Abulfazl, and while he was still a young man.

But for every such act of violence, a score of wise and humane enactments can be cited.

In the seventh year of his reign it was decreed that the wives and children of soldiers captured in war should no longer be made slaves; in the eighth the onerous taxes on pilgrims were removed; in the ninth the poll-tax on unbelievers (a mighty multitude) was abolished;* in the twenty-fifth a full census of all the inhabitants (giving names and occupations) was made, in order to equalize the incidence of taxation; in the twenty-eighth the obligatory *suttee* was abolished, and Akbar himself broke up the custom by his personal presence; these, among many other instances, may be cited.

"He was a powerful, world-subduing monarch, the very emblem of justice. His object was to unite all men in a common bond of

---

* A century before Akbar's time the Muhammadan ruler of Cashmere—Ali Shah—had anticipated many of Akbar's reforms in dealing with his Hindu subjects. He abolished the hated tax on infidels, forbade the slaughter of oxen, and was, besides, an ardent patron of learning and of the arts. These and other like matters were familiar to Akbar through verbal reports and, after the twelfth year of his reign, through the translation of the history of Cashmere which Faizi was preparing. The doctrine of universal toleration, too, was no new thing in India. During the whole of the sixteenth century it was preached and practised by the Sikhs.

peace." He strove to be the king of *all* his subjects. He maintained four hundred and fifteen *Mansebdars*—commanders of horse. Of these, fifty-one were Hindus, the rest Moguls, Usbeks, Afghans, Turks, and Persians. Shah Jahan had six hundred and nine *Mansebdars*, of whom one hundred and ten were Hindus. It was simply impossible to govern these chiefs and their followers by the rigid law of Islam. Tolerance was a political necessity. As Lord Tennyson has said in the notes to his poem of *Akbar's Dream*, "His tolerance of religion, and his abhorrence of religious persecutions, put our Tudors to shame."

The most interesting incidents of his reign are connected with the foundation of "the Divine Monotheism." His chief adviser in this step was his *wazir* Abul-fazl.

Shaikh Mubarak, a distinguished and liberal-minded scholar, had two yet more distinguished and liberal-minded sons—Faizi the poet (born 1547), and Abul-fazl the writer, the statesman, and the prime minister of Akbar (born 1551). It is necessary to know something of this family, whose influence was predominant during the larger part of Akbar's life. Faizi was first introduced at court in the twelfth year of Akbar's reign, and became his friend and favorite. Abul-fazl came six years later, in 1574, when Akbar, now thirty-two years old, began to have some respite from his incessant wars and expeditions. Shaikh Mubarak was bred an orthodox *Sunni*, had become, more or less, a *Shia*, and had investigated the various religions of India and of Persia.

Faizi's poems often turn on religious questions, which are sometimes treated mystically, but frequently in a spirit of simple devotion. Like all poets, he deals with the universal passion of love; but, as with other Orientals, it is the beautiful boy who is the beloved. Abul-fazl promises at some future time to give a critical edition of Faizi's verses;* "but now," he says, "but now, it is brotherly love—a love which does not travel along the road of critical nicety—that commands me to write down some of his verses."

* A promise which he redeemed.

I shall copy a few of the many extracts so given, partly to illustrate the nature of the poetry of the age, partly to exhibit the character of the poet, and that of the emperor who admired and loved him.

These verses are from Faizi's *Odes:*

Oh Thou who existest from Eternity, and abidest forever, sight cannot bear Thy light, praise cannot express Thy perfection.

Thy light melts the understanding, and Thy glory baffles wisdom; to think of Thee destroys reason; Thy essence confounds thought.

Science is like blinding desert sand on the road to Thy perfection; the town of Literature is a mere hamlet compared with the world of Thy knowledge.

Human knowledge and thought combined can only spell the first letter of the alphabet of Thy love.

Each brain is full of the thought of grasping Thee; the brow of Plato even burned with the fever heat of this hopeless thought.

Oh man, thou coin bearing the double stamp of body and spirit, I do not know what thy nature is; for thou art higher than heaven and lower than earth.

Thy frame contains the image of the heavenly and the lower regions; be either heavenly or earthly, thou art at liberty to choose.

Do not act against thy reason, for it is a trustworthy counsellor; put not thy heart on illusions, for the heart is a lying fool.

Be ashamed of thy appearance; for thou pridest thyself on the title of "sum-total," and art yet but a marginal note.

If thou wishest to understand the secret meaning of the phrase "to prefer the welfare of others to thy own," treat thyself with poison and others with sugar.

My dear Son, consider how short the time is that the star of good fortune revolves according to thy wish; Fate shows no friendship.

The companion of my loneliness is my comprehensive genius; the scratching of my pen is harmony for my ear.

If I were to bring forth what is in my mind, I wonder whether the spirit of the age could bear it.

The following couplets are from the *Ghazals*:

It were better if I melted my heart, and laid the foundation for a new one; I have too often patiently patched up my torn heart.

Although life far from thee is an approach to death, yet to stand at a distance is a mark of courtesy.

I cannot show ungratefulness to Love. Has he not overwhelmed me with—sadness and sadness?

I cannot understand the juggler-trick which love performed; it introduced Thy form through so small an aperture as the pupil of my eye, into the large space of my heart, and yet my heart cannot contain it.

The most wonderful thing I have seen is Faizi's heart; it is at once the pearl, the ocean, and the diver.

This verse from the *Rubais* goes very far in flattery of the emperor:

If you wish to see the path of guidance as I have done, you will never see it without having seen the king.
Thy old-fashioned prostration is of no advantage to thee—see Akbar and you see God.

Akbar had been, in all outward respects at least, a good Muslim up to the year 1574, making pilgrimages to the tombs of saints, etc.* Unquestionably his mind had been revolving religious doubts for some time previous. The influence of Abul-fazl seems to have confirmed Akbar's disposition, and to have stimulated definite inquiry.

Shah Nawaz Khan (born 1699), a standard authority, says of him that "It has often been asserted that Abul-fazl was an infidel; it is more just to say that he was a pantheist. There is no doubt that he was a man of lofty character, and desired to live at peace with all men." He was magnanimous to his enemies; he was pure in his mind; he was incorruptibly honest in the public service. Abul-fazl was an elegant writer. "His pen was more feared than

* In the twelfth year of his reign he destroyed or mutilated the fine monuments of Chitor, partly for political reasons, no doubt; but partly, also, for religious ones.

Akbar's arrow." He was an excellent administrator, a loyal and devoted subject, a liberal patron, a considerate friend. A large share of the glory of Akbar's reign is directly due to him. Such a king deserved such a *wazir*.

Bedauni (one of the emperor's historians, and a man of learning) says of Abul-fazl, that Akbar "looked upon him more favorably than he did upon me;" that Abul-fazl "ingratiated himself by his unremitting devotion to the king's service, by his temporizing disposition, by his duplicity, by his study of the king's sentiments, and by his boundless flattery." Abul-fazl's flattery was boundless at times, but not more so than the habit of the age demanded. He was never silly about it, like the courtier who told *Le Roi-Soleil* that the rain at Marly was not wet. Abul-fazl's fortunes (deservedly) rose till he became *wazir*. "But poor I," says Bedauni, "from my inexperience and simplicity, could not manage to advance myself." "I do not like my position, and should be glad to be in any other." He himself was much to blame for his ill-fortune, as he made enemies right and left, and was so foolish as to be absent from his duties for a long time without a leave. The king did not like him (though his learning was doubtless appreciated), and on one occasion spoke harshly to him at court. "From that day," Bedauni says, "I have abandoned my presumptuous and controversial manner." Both Abul-fazl and his distinguished brother Faizi were constantly kind to Bedauni for a space of forty years. He was never tired of reviling them, partly, no doubt, from sheer envy of their success. It is only fair to say, however, that he was a truly devout Muhammadan, and that his religious beliefs were daily outraged by the doings and sayings of these free-thinking heretics.

Poor Bedauni was set (much against his will) to translate the *Maha-Bharata* for the emperor's library. What a task for a true believer! "The consequence was, that I translated two sections, at the puerile absurdities of which the creation may well be amazed. Such injunctions as one never heard of! What *not* to eat, and a prohibition against turnips!" "But such is my fate—to be employed on such works!" "Abul-fazl wrote the preface. Allah defend us from his infidelities and absurdities!" Bedauni also translated the *Ramayana*, spending four years in the task. He seems to have been better pleased with this work, for, when he presented the complete book, "it was greatly praised." We learn that a Jesuit from Goa translated many Greek treatises for the emperor's library.

The *Ain-i-Akbari* of Abul-fazl presents the history of Akbar's change of religious opinions from the view-point of one who was himself high-priest of the new religion. The *wazir* of Akbar puts the most favorable construction upon every circumstance.

The native historians also contain many references to the establishment of the Divine Faith, and the more important extracts shall be copied here. Professor Blochmann's edition of Abul-fazl's work devotes a long note of fifty pages to a history of Akbar's religious views. It is very largely composed of extracts from Bedauni; and these extracts are carefully arranged in chronological order. Bedauni was certainly a prejudiced witness and a disappointed courtier; but he was, no less certainly, a man of intelligence, learning, and courage. Allowance should be made for his bias; but his testimony deserves the most careful attention. I shall extract from Professor Blochmann's translation of Bedauni the most significant paragraphs, in order to present both sides of a most important question. Akbar is too great a man to need any praise that is not his just due.

"It was during these days (A.D. 1574) that Abul-fazl came the second time to court. He laid before the emperor (as a present) a commentary on (one of the verses of the Kuran); and, though people said that it had been written by his father, Abul-fazl was much praised."

Bedauni now gives an account of the persecutions to which Abul-fazl and his two sons had been subjected in the early years of Akbar's reign. They were not orthodox *Sunnis*, and they had been obliged to fly for their lives and to keep in hiding for safety. Faizi had been called to court as a poet, and had been received graciously on that account, as has been said. His influence over Akbar grew rapidly and surely; and soon his father and his younger brother were high in Akbar's favor through their own merits and on his introduction. They did not persecute their early enemies.

"During the year 1575 many places of worship were built by command of his majesty. The cause was this. For many years previously the emperor had gained remarkable and decisive victories. The empire had grown in extent from day to day; everything had turned out well. His majesty had thus leisure . . . and passed much of his time in discussing the Kuran and the Traditions. Sufism, scientific discussions, inquiries into philosophy and law, were the order of the day. His majesty passed whole nights in thoughts of God; his heart was full of reverence for Him who is the true Giver. From a feeling of thankfulness for his past successes, he would sit many a morning alone, in prayer and melancholy, on a large flat stone which lay near the palace, in a lonely spot, with his head bent over his chest, gathering the bliss of early hours."

"The emperor had, from his youth, taken delight in the society of learned men. He always treated them with respect and honor. He listened to their discussions of nice points of science, of the ancient and modern history of religions and peoples and sects, and he profited by what he heard." He built a special palace for such assemblies in the twentieth year of his reign (when he was thirty-three years old), and spent many nights there in their company. The palace had four halls. In the western, the descendants of the Prophet sat; in the southern, sat the learned and the wise; in the northern, the *Shaikhs* and "men-of-ecstasy;" in the eastern, the nobles of the court who were in sympathy with learning. When his majesty was too fatigued with business to attend these meetings, he sent one of his nobles in his place, choosing a man "in whose kindness and gentleness he had confidence."

Some idea of the constitution of Akbar's court, and of the wise men who assembled in these congresses, can be obtained from the biographies given at the end of Bedauni's history, which relate to thirty-eight *Shaikhs* and holy men, sixty-nine "learned men," fifteen physicians, and no less than one hundred and fifty-three poets. The names of three monks who lived at court have come down to us—Rudolpho Aquaviva, Antonio de Monserrato, Francisco Enriques. These meetings for discussion were held every Thursday night. They were fully attended, and they were often very far from orderly. "The Chief Justice, in the meeting-hall, called Hadji Ibrahim an accursed wretch, and lifted up his stick to strike him."

Muhammad predicted that Islam would be divided into seventy-two heretical sects; and there were representatives of enough hostile parties in these meetings to bring their discussions to violent terminations. Akbar became frankly disgusted with what he saw and heard in his meeting-hall. Abul-fazl, his father, and his brother, did not fail to point out the scandal of it to the emperor, though, at first, it appears they did not join freely in the disputes.

Akbar's disgust was the first stage in his perversion from Islam. He soon went farther. On one occasion he commanded the presence of a high doctor of the law, "as he wished to annoy him." Abul-fazl and some others newly come to court were set on by the emperor to oppose him. "His majesty took every occasion to interrupt." According to an order previously given by Akbar, some of those present began to tell scandalous stories of the invited guest, and to badger him in many offensive ways. The doctor was disgraced, and odium was thrown on the cause which he represented. At a later meeting, Akbar, who had as many wives as Solomon,* set a trap for the Muslim doctors of the law by asking how many free-born wives he could lawfully maintain. There is no doubt that the maximum number for a good Muslim is four. Muslim practice has always winked

* The *names* of eleven wives are given by Blochmann. There were five thousand women in the harem, including servants.

at an unlimited number of wives for kings; but Akbar put the question as a matter of Muslim theory. If he could have but four wives, what, then, was the legal status of the many free-born and high-born Rajput princesses in his harem? Were they concubines? Dare the Muhammadan doctors insult the emperor's wives? The trap was not a fair one. The Muslim doctor who was the victim on that occasion, closed his part of the discussion with a very sensible remark, when he saw that the case was hopeless. "Very well," said he, "I have nothing more to add; just as his majesty pleases." A complaisant *Cazi* was found who, then and there, gave a decree that such marriages were legal. "The veteran lawyers made very long faces at these proceedings," as well they might. The most uncompromising of the religious orthodox were now banished; new heretics came to court and were received into favor, and new heresies sprung up. "His majesty had the early history of Islam read to him, and soon commenced to think less well" of everything concerned with it. "Soon after, the observance of the five prayers and fasts, and the belief in everything connected with the Prophet, were put down as religious blindness, and man's reason was acknowledged as the basis of all religion. Portuguese priests also came frequently, and his majesty inquired into the articles of their belief, which are based on reason."

In the year 1576 Bedauni again chronicles the arrival of new heretics. The Thursday evening discussions still continued, and became more and more violent. The fundamental truths of Islam were now called in question.

In 1578 Bedauni writes: "His majesty, till now, had shown every sincerity, and was diligently searching for truth. But his education had been much neglected; and, surrounded as he was by men of low and heretic principles, he had been forced to doubt the truth of Islam. Falling from one perplexity into the other, he lost sight of his real object, the search for truth; and when the strong embankment of our clear law and our excellent faith had once been broken through, his majesty grew colder and colder, till, after the short space of five or six years, not a trace of Muhammadan feeling was left in his heart. Matters then became very different."

In 1595 Bedauni says matters had come to such a pass that a request to make the pilgrimage to Mecca would have subjected the asker to capital punishment.

"A faith based on some elementary principles traced itself (gradually) on the mirror of his heart, and there grew the conviction that there were sensible men in all religions (and in all ages). If some true knowledge was thus everywhere to be found, why should truth be confined to one religion; or to a creed like Islam, which was scarcely a thousand years old?"

"The doctrine of the transmigration of souls, especially, took deep root in his heart." Flatterers told the emperor that "the perfect man" referred to the ruler of the age, and that the nature of a king was holy. "In this way many agreeable things were said to the emperor." "Learned monks brought the gospel. His majesty firmly believed in the truth of the Christian religion, and ordered Prince Murad (then eight years old) to take a few lessons in Christianity." "These accursed monks applied the description of a cursed Satan to Muhammad, the best of all prophets—God's blessings rest on him and his whole house—a thing which even devils would not do." The Brahmin Rajah Bir Bal "impressed upon the emperor that the sun was the origin of everything. The emperor learned, from some Hindus, formularies to reduce the influence of the sun to his subjection, and read them morning and evening as a religious exercise." The sun was venerated as the chief light and benefactor of the world, and as a friend to kings, who used it to mark periods and eras.

Akbar next prohibited the slaughter of cows, for two reasons; first, "because the Hindus devoutly worship them," and, second, "because physicians represent their flesh as difficult of digestion and productive of illness" (as it very likely is in the hot climate of India). Akbar was eminently practical in his religious enactments, while he was at the same time devout. "Although he had full trust and hope of heavenly assistance, he neglected no material means of success," says one of his officials.

Fire-worshippers also came to the court and taught their religion, and the sacred fire (lighted with a lens at the vernal equinox) was committed to the care of Abulfazl. "Fire is one of the signs of God," said the emperor, "and one light from among the many lights of his creation." "In the twenty-fifth year of his reign he prostrated himself before the sun in public; and in the evening the whole court had to rise up respectfully when the lamps were lighted." "These sentiments had been long growing in the emperor's mind, and ripened gradually to a firm conviction."

"In the year 1579 his majesty was anxious to unite in his person the powers of the state and those of the church, for he could not bear to be subordinate to any one." He made an attempt to read the public prayers in the mosque, ending with some verses of Faizi's:

> *The Lord has given me the empire,*
> *And a wise heart, and a strong arm.*
> *He has guided me in righteousness and justice,*
> *And has removed from my thoughts everything but justice.*
> *His praise surpasses man's understanding,*
> *Great is his power, Allahu Akbar!*

Fear or the hope of promotion continually brought new converts to Akbar's views.

In the year 1579 Akbar issued a proclamation which declared his judgments to be of higher validity than those of the religious doctors, and which virtually pronounced him to be infallible.* If there were a variance of opinion upon questions of religion, the decree of the king was to be final and binding. "Further, if his majesty, in his unerring judgment, should issue an order which is not in opposition to the Kuran, and which is for the benefit of the nation, it shall be

---

* He had previously obtained the sanction of the doctors of the law, for form's sake. The document which they (reluctantly) signed made the emperor the spiritual as well as the temporal chief of the nation. "The intellect of the just king" took the place of the Kuran as the basis of the law.

binding and imperative on every man; opposition to it shall involve damnation in the world to come, and loss of religion and property in this life."

"His majesty had now determined to use the formula: 'There is no God beside God, and Akbar is God's representative;' but as he found that the extravagance of this led to contentions, he restricted the use of it to a few people in the harem."

In this same eventful year the emperor "distinctly denied the existence of *jinns*, of angels, and of all other beings of the invisible world, as well as the miracles of the prophets and the saints; he rejected the testimony of the witnesses of our faith, the proofs of the Kuran, the existence of the soul after death and future rewards and punishments so far as they differed from metempsychosis." Later on, his partisans strenuously insisted on the miracles performed by Akbar; but they were feeble matters at the best—he spoke at his birth, was one—and carried no conviction.

Muslims, but Akbar ordered the officers of his court to appear with shaven faces. This was in the year 1592, when he was fifty years old.*

Akbar became more and more ready to claim the dignity of a prophet, or even divine honors, says Bedauni. He also became intolerant of opposition, and deported good (and stubborn) Muslims as slaves, exchanging them for Turkish horses. "His majesty was now (1582) convinced that the millennium was drawing near." The coinage was changed to show the era of the millennium; a history of the past thousand years was written; it was ordered that prostrations should be made before the king. Wine

* I have, however, a beautiful portrait of him, in which he wears a white beard, parted and brushed sidewise in the Hindu fashion. It must have been painted late in his life. The face is nervous, almost querulous in expression, fine to the verge of anxiousness. In middle life his face was strong and somewhat coarse. Portraits, taken in his last years, represent him with a long white moustache and a full beard closely clipped. A medal struck after his death represents him without a beard. I have never been fortunate enough to see a picture of Akbar in his youth.

† We may recall that Europe in A.D. 1000 was subject to like delusions.

shops were licensed in Agra. Pigs and dogs were no longer looked on as unclean. A splendid tomb was even built for one of Akbar's hounds. Certain of the ceremonial ablutions were abrogated. It was forbidden to marry a cousin. The prayers of Islam and the pilgrimage were prohibited. The era of the *Hegira* was abolished. A new Persian solar year was introduced. The feasts of the Zoroastrians were revived. The Jesuits of Agra and Lahore exhibited representations of the birth of Christ in wax. "In the same way every doctrine of Islam was doubted and ridiculed." "The good were in fear, and the wicked were secure." "His majesty saw in the defeat of one party a proof of his own infallibility." One of the Muslim Mullas wrote, in derision:

This year the emperor has claimed prophetship,
Next year, if God wills, he will be God.

Everything did not go smoothly with Akbar, however. Many of the best men held aloof. Rajah Bhagwan said to the emperor: "Only tell us where the new sect is, so that I may believe." Rajah Man Singh declared that Islam he knew, and Hinduism he knew, but besides these he knew no other religion. One of the courtiers had made his fortune by proposing to introduce the custom of prostration before the king. Another, with an eye to profit, exclaimed, "Oh that I had been the inventor of this little business!" A devout Muslim courtier used to say his prayers in the audience chamber. When Akbar asked him to say them at home, he replied: "My king, this is not your kingdom, that you should give orders." Whereupon Akbar called him a fool, and cancelled his grant of land.

In 1583 new orders of various kinds were made to "please the Hindus." Akbar wore the Hindu mark on his forehead, and the Brahminic thread. "His majesty learned alchemy, and showed in public some of the gold made by him." "Cheating Brahmins collected a set of a thousand and one Sanscrit names of his majesty the Sun, and told the emperor that he was an incarnation like *Ram* and others. They also brought

Sanscrit verses, said to have been taken from the sayings of ancient sages, in which it was predicted that a great conqueror should rise up in India who would honor Brahmins and cows, and govern the world with justice. They wrote this nonsense on old-looking paper and showed it to the emperor, who believed every word of it."

Bedauni carries the history farther, with new details, but in what has gone before he has said his say; the side of the good Muslim has been presented well and vigorously. Professor Blochmann sums up the evidence in a few words, saying that it shows how "Akbar, starting from the idea of the divine right of kings, gradually came to look upon himself as the (high priest) of the age, then as the prophet of God and God's vicegerent on earth, and lastly as a deity."

We have an account of the king's change of religious opinions, from Shaikh Nuru-l-Hakh. "One of the strange incidents of this year (1578) was the king's abandonment of the national religion, which became a stumbling-block to many people weak in the faith." The king was constantly in attendance at the assemblies for religious discussion, "for his mind was solely bent on ascertaining the truth." "The common people learning, day after day, something of the nature of the subjects discussed in these assemblies, entertained suspicions of the king's motives, which were derogatory to his character and but little deserved." They, in fact, feared that Akbar would assume divine honors, as he subsequently did, so far as was politic, or even possible.

Abul-fazl's account of the discussion of the wise men is interesting. He says: "Sufis, doctors, preachers, lawyers, Sunnis, Shias, Brahmans, Buddhists, Christians, Jews, Zoroastrians, and learned men of every belief were gathered together in the royal assembly. Each one fearlessly brought forward his assertions, and the contentions were long and heated." A Jesuit from Goa refuted all comers, and offered, "with perfect calmness and earnest conviction," to undergo the ordeal of the fiery furnace with the Bible in his hands, against the Muhammedan doctors with the Kuran. The challenge was refused with angry words. The emperor also made experiments in natural religion. "It was ordered that some twenty suckling infants should be kept in a secluded place where they should not hear a word spoken, so as to test the accuracy of the tradition which says, 'Every one is born with an inclination to religion.'" This experiment was to see what creed they would incline to. It came to naught, for "after three or four years the children all came out dumb." The experiment may have been suggested by Herodotus' account of a similar experience, which led to equally unsatisfactory conclusions.

The following judgment, written by Mr. Sherar, C.S.I., presents a view of Akbar's religious experiments which it is worth while to quote. It is not the received view of Akbar's character, and it certainly is not a complete account. On the other hand, there is a shade of truth in it, at the very least. It should be weighed along with the rest.

Mr. Sherar says: "Akbar was more amused at new doctrines, new theories, new objects of veneration, than burdened with the difficulties which surrounded the acceptance of them. And there surely is no parallel between a grave and powerful mind bowed down, everlastingly, with the stern dilemmas of that great enigma, whence and whither? and the superficial curiosity of an intellect that was too restless to bind itself permanently to any particular code of opinions."

For my own part, I have found no brief judgment of Akbar's faith so entirely satisfactory as that of Elphinstone, who says: "It is to his internal policy that Akbar owes his place in that highest order of princes, whose reigns have been a blessing to mankind; and that policy shows itself in different shapes, as it affects religious or civil government. Akbar's tolerant spirit was displayed early in his reign, and appears to have been entirely independent of any doubts of the divine origin of the Muhammadan faith. It led him, however, to listen, without prejudice, to the doctrines of other religions, and involved him in enmity with the bigoted members of his own, and must thus have contributed to shake his early belief, and to dispose him to question the infallible authority of the Kuran. The political advantages of a new religion, which should take in all classes of his subjects, could not fail, moreover, to occur to him. In the first part of his reign he was assiduous in visiting sacred places, and in attendance on holy men; even in the twenty-first year of his reign he spoke seriously of performing the pilgrimage to Mecca. . . . The religion of Akbar seems to have been pure Deism, in addition to which some ceremonies were permitted in consideration of human infirmity. It maintained that we ought to reverence God according to the knowledge of him derived from our own reason, by which his unity and benevolence are sufficiently established; that we ought to serve him and to seek for our future happiness by subduing our bad passions and practising such virtues as are beneficial to mankind; but that we should not adopt a creed on the authority of *any man*, as all were liable to vice and error like ourselves. If it were absolutely necessary for men to have some visible object of adoration, by means of which they might raise their souls to the Divinity, Akbar recommended that the sun, the planets, or fire should be the symbols. He had no priests, no public worship, and no restrictions about food, except a recommendation of abstinence, as tending to exalt the mind. His only observances were salutations to the sun, prayers at midnight and daybreak, and meditations at noon on the sun. . . . But as Akbar *practised* all his ceremonies, as well as permitted them, it may be doubted whether they had not gained some hold on his imagination. He seems to have been by nature devout, and, with all his scepticism, to have inclined even to superstitions that promised him a closer connection with the Deity." It is necessary to pause for a moment and to remark that, while these judgments are eminently true, we are trying this ruler of the sixteenth century by the standards of our own day. It is wonderful how the test is met.

"In these days (A.D. 1575–76), his majesty asked how it would be if he engraved the words *Allahu-Akbar* (which means *God is great*, but which can be made to mean *Akbar is God*) upon the imperial coins." The ambiguity was pointed out to him, and he was displeased, saying that "it was self-evident that no creature, in the depths of his impotence, could advance any claim to divinity." The words were, however, finally so engraved.

Of Akbar's revenue arrangements we have this account by Bedauni (who was a malcontent): "Regulations were circulated, but eventually these were not observed as they ought to have been." He admits the excellence of the regulations themselves, but gives instances where the peasants' lands were laid waste, and their wives and children sold through the rapacity of the officials. But "many of the officials were brought to account" and punished; even tortured. In spite of this, the fate of the husbandman and of the soldier was hard; "but for all this, the emperor's good fortune was so great and flourishing, that his enemies were everywhere annihilated, and soldiers were not so much wanted." One of the Sivaite poets of Bengal (quoted by Sir W. W. Hunter) in the sixteenth century, gives a life-like picture of the oppressions of Muhammadan officers in the remoter districts of the empire. "All classes," he says, "were crushed with an equal tyranny; fallow lands were entered as arable; and, by a false measurement, three-fourths of a *bigha* were taxed as a full *bigha*. The treasury officers deducted more than one rupee in seven, short weight and exchange. The husbandmen fled from their lands and threw their cattle and goods into the markets, so that 'a rupee's worth of things sold for ten annas.'"

In another native authority we read: "At this place some of the emperor's officers were directed to protect the cultivated land in the vicinity of the camp; and, besides this, trustworthy men were directed to carefully examine the land after the army had passed and to assess the damage done. This practice became a rule in all his campaigns." * It is plain that the effort of the emperor was to do justice. It is certain that the older provinces of the kingdom were well and mildly governed. It is beyond a doubt that frequent instances of misrule and oppression occurred everywhere, especially in the newly conquered districts. It was obviously necessary for Akbar to be tolerant in religious matters for the sake of political stability. How much of his even-handed justice and mild benevolence sprang from the same necessity, it is not possible to say. But leaving to one side all questions as to interior motives, the writings of the native historians show that the emperor's reign was marked by the most consummate political skill. His personal character is far less engaging and distinguished than that of his grandfather Babar; he did not leave so many magnificent buildings as Shah Jahan; but he con-

* The troops of the Fronde (1652) regularly pillaged the quarters of Paris which they chanced to hold, precisely as if they had been in the heart of an enemy's country.

solidated a great state by wise, just, and even generous laws, and left a homogeneous empire behind him. We are used to represent to ourselves the kingdom of the Great Mogul as a barbaric state, ruled by a semi-fabulous monster of bloodthirsty disposition. A more careful inspection shows us an empire which will bear close comparison with the states of Europe at the same epoch. The blood of Timur had been thinned so that it ran calmly in the veins of a great statesman and a good king, and the lust of mere conquest was replaced by a sincere desire for "the happiness and prosperity of the husbandman."

The character of the Mogul invaders of India in Timur's day is indicated in the first chapter of this book. Their acts portray them. The history of Babar, six generations later, sufficiently displays the high ideals of culture which were held by the chief men of his time. Music, oratory, poetry, were cultivated even by sanguinary military leaders. They maintained at their courts, painters, architects, musicians, astronomers. The doctors of the religious law were learned in the fashion of the time, speculative and eloquent. Arabian ideals of military chivalry prevailed, or had begun to prevail. Akbar opened the road of promotion to all the nations of Western Asia. Persians, Afghans, Turkis, Hindus, were welcome at his court, and all were on equal terms. In intellectual matters this intermixture of races and religions showed itself in great freedom and liberality in ideals of culture. Every famous book from the *Shah-Nameh* to the *Mahabharata* was in Akbar's library. In religious questions a revolution was accomplished. The standards of military chivalry, which had been based on Turki and Arab models, were modified by the customs of the splendid Rajput soldiers.

These processes went on during the reigns of Jahangir and of Shah Jahan. It was not until the reign of Aurangzeb that they received a check. We must figure to ourselves the period between Akbar and Aurangzeb as one of remarkable freedom. I suppose the peasants' condition was not especially different from what it now is. But the host of officials, great and small, military and civil, were free to do or to think as they liked, provided, only, that they performed their duties fairly well, paid their regular tribute to the king, and did not meddle with plots against their rulers. No one interfered with their doings, and no one troubled himself about the opinions of his neighbors. There was no "non-conformist conscience," and no Inquisition to be taken account of by any man. When Aurangzeb came to the throne, this happy state of things was changed, and the rigid law of Islam became the rule of conduct, as we shall see; but India was under liberal rule during the years 1556–1658.

CHAPTER V

JAHANGIR, EMPEROR OF HINDUSTAN (A.D. 1605–1627)

A Contribution towards a Natural History of Tyrants

But if Cæsar, the emperor, should adopt you, no one could endure your arrogance.—EPICTETUS.

THE most interesting authority on the reign and character of this prince is the *Diary of Sir Thomas Roe*, English Envoy to his court from James the First. The narrative has real literary merits, and is inspired by a sound good sense. The contrast of the characters of the emperor and the envoy, who esteemed each other, is most marked and most interesting. Sir Thomas's *Journal* commences as follows; his very words are given when it is practicable:

"March the 16th (1615) we lost sight of the Lizard; the 26th we saw the coast of Barbary; April the 14th we cut the line; and on the 5th of June came to anchor in the bay of Saldanha, next the Cape of Good Hope." From thence the voyage continued till, on the 26th of September, Sir Thomas landed at Surat, where the British East India Company had its factory. Here he "continued till the 30th of October, suffering much from the (native) governor, who, by force, searched many chests and took out what he thought fit." On this day the envoy departed on his land journey to the capital of the Great Mogul. His mission was to conclude a treaty of commerce, and to collect outstanding debts due to English merchants. How important the commerce of England with India was becoming, may be read in Mill's history. The profits were immense. Eight voyages in the years 1603–1613 yielded an *average* of 171 per cent.* By the 14th of November Sir Thomas had reached Brampore, which he guessed to be two hundred and twenty-three miles beyond

* Tavernier says that the profits of the Portuguese were 500 or even 1000 per cent.

Surat. Here he was met by an officer of the king, who conducted him to his lodgings in the town, which were "four chambers like ovens, and no bigger, made of brick in the side of a wall, so that I lay in my tent; the officer making his excuse that it was the best lodging in the town, as I found it was."

"I was conducted to visit the prince (Parwiz, a son of the emperor), in whose outward court I found about a hundred gentlemen on horseback. He sat high in a gallery that went around. An officer told me that as I approached I must touch the ground with my head, which I refused, and went on to a place right under him, railed in, where I made him reverence, and he bowed his body; so I went within, where were all the great men of the town, with their hands before them like slaves. The place was covered overhead with a rich canopy, and under foot all with carpets. It was like a great stage, and the prince sat at the upper end of it. Having no place assigned me, I stood right before him, he refusing to admit me to come up the steps or to allow me a chair. Having received my presents, he offered to go into another room where I should be allowed to sit; but, by the way, he made himself drunk out of a case of bottles I gave him, and so the visit ended." This was our envoy's first struggle with Indian etiquette, and here, as always after, he stood up mightily for the dignity of an ambassador of the King of England. The termination of the ceremony was not unusual either for prince or emperor. From his meeting with the prince, Sir Thomas proceeded on his journey, passing through the country of the Rajah Rama, "who is lineally descended from Porus, that warlike Indian monarch overcome by Alexander the Great."

On January 10, 1616, he had arrived at the court of Jahangir, and presented himself at the *durbar* (audience) at four in the afternoon. Here "the Mogul sits daily to entertain strangers, receive petitions and presents, give out orders, and to see and be seen. And here it will be proper to give some account of his court."

"None but eunuchs come within the king's

private lodgings, and his women, who guard him with warlike weapons. The Mogul every morning shows himself to the common people at a window. At noon he is there again to see elephants and wild beasts fight, the men of rank being under him within a rail. After noon he comes to the *durbar* aforementioned. After the supper, at eight of the clock, he comes down to the *Guzalcan*, a fair court, in the midst of which is a throne of freestone, where he sits. Here he discourses of indifferent things very affably. No business of state is done anywhere but at one of these places, where it is publicly canvassed, and so registered, which register may be seen for two shillings, and the common people know as much as the council, so that every day the king's resolutions are the public news, and exposed to the censure of every scoundrel."

"Before my audience I had obtained leave to use the customs of my country. At the *durbar* I was conducted right before him; entering the outward rail, two noble slaves met to conduct me nearer. At the first rail

I made a low reverence, at the next another, and when under the king a third. His reception was very favorable, but does not need particularizing."

"When I came in I found him sitting cross-legged on a little throne, all clad in diamonds, pearls, and rubies, before him a table of gold, on it about fifty pieces of gold plate, set all with stones, his nobility about him in their best equipages, whom he commanded to drink, froliquely, several wines standing by in great flagons. So drinking and commanding others, his majesty and all his lords became the finest men I ever saw—of a thousand humours."

Apparently the business of the envoy did not advance. "March the first I rid out to see a house of pleasure of the king's, seated between two mighty rocks, and defended from the sun. It is a place of melancholy, delight, and safety." On the 11th of March began the festival of the New Year, when great presents of all sorts were offered to the king, which, though not equal to report, were yet incredible enough. On the 12th of March came another audience, and on the 13th another, when "I pressed to have the peace and commerce with England settled after a solemn manner, which the Mogul ordered should be done." It may be noted here that delay in attending to the missions of envoys and in dismissing them was considered a proof of the king's dignity, and that it was many a long day before Sir Thomas had his treaty signed and the debts due the English merchants settled.

"On the 23d the Mogul condemned one of his own nation on suspicion of felony, and sent him to me in irons, as a slave, to dispose of at my will. This is looked upon as a great favor, for which I returned thanks; adding that in England we had no slaves, nor thought it lawful to make the image of God equal to a beast, but that I would use him as a servant, and if he behaved himself well, give him his liberty. This the Mogul was well pleased with." On this, as on every other occasion, the English envoy conducted himself with sense, and with a simple dignity which evidently impressed the autocrat, who was never tired of showing him marks of his appreciation.

One must read the original narrative in all its detail to obtain the full sense of the dramatic contrast between these two men of different countries, whose mutual respect was founded on something deeper than race.

At one of the *durbars*, Sir Thomas stood alone in a high place of honor. "Asaph-Chan (the king's brother-in-law) insisted that I should rank myself among the nobility. I refused at first, but then removed to the other side, where only the prince and young Rama were, which more disgusted Asaph-Chan." A complaint to the king was of no avail, "so I kept my place in quiet." "On the 31st of March, the king dined at Asaph-Chan's house, all the way from the palace to it, which was an English mile, being laid under foot with silks and velvets sewed together, but rolled up as the king passed. They reported that the feast and present cost £150,000." Little progress was made in the business, as usual.

"On June 18th, the king commanded one

of his brother's sons, who had been persuaded to become a Christian, with a design to make him odious to the people (so says Sir Thomas), to lay his hand on the head of a lion that was brought before the king, which he refused out of fear; upon which the king bid his youngest son go touch the lion, who did so without receiving any hurt. Whereat the king took occasion to send his nephew away to prison, where he is never like to see daylight."*

In July a gentlewoman of Nur-Mahal's was punished for a breach of decorum. "The poor woman was set up to the armpits in the earth close rammed about her, with her feet tied to a stake, so to continue three days and two nights. If she died not in that time she was to be pardoned."

"On August the 9th, a hundred thieves were brought chained before the Mogul, with their accusation; without further ceremony

---

* Four of Jahangir's nephews were baptized by the Jesuits by the names of Philippo, Carlo, Henrico, Eduardo; and the doors of the palace at Lahore bore "the images of the crucifix and of the Blessed Virgin," so says Herbert in his Travels.

he ordered them to be carried away, the chief of them to be torn in pieces by dogs, the rest put to death. This was all the process and form," and the sentence was carried out.

"Seven months were now spent in soliciting the signing and sealing of the articles of peace and commerce, and nothing obtained but promises from week to week and from day to day." During October the envoy recites some of the struggles between the king's sons for power at court. The wisest men foresee a civil war upon the king's death. "The whole court is full of whispers; the nobility are sad; the multitude, like itself, full of rumor and noise, without head or order, rages, but applies not to any proper means."

Sir Thomas says: "The history of this country for variety of matter and the many subtle practices in the time of Akbar-Shah, the father of this king, were well worth writing; but because they come from such remote parts, many will despise them; and by reason these people are esteemed barbarous, few will believe them; and therefore I forbear making them public, though I could deliver as many rare and notable acts of state, subtle evasions, policies, answers and adages, as I believe, for one age, would not easily be equalled." It is a loss not to have had this history from so good an observer.

About this time came the ambassador of Persia, who was obliged to make the "knocking his head against the ground," which Sir Thomas had refused to do. "He brought for presents three times nine Arabian and Persian horses, this being a ceremonious number among them; nine mules very fair and large; seven camels laden with velvet; two chests of Persian hangings; one rich cabinet; forty muskets; five clocks; one camel laden with cloth of gold; eight carpets of silk; two rubies; twenty-one camel loads of wine; fourteen camel loads of distilled sweet waters; seven of rose water; seven daggers set with precious stones; five swords set after the same manner; seven Venetian looking-glasses, and these so fair and rich that I was out of countenance when I heard it." In fact, the meanness of the presents which Sir Thomas had brought from England was a constant thorn in his side. Only the large mastiff-dogs seem to have been thoroughly appreciated; and the emperor told him plainly that he could not understand why the monarch of so great a country as England should send so poor a list of presents.

It is easily to be seen that the real success of Sir Thomas' mission was due to his personality, and not to the fame of England or to the value of his gifts.

"These people know the best of all kinds of merchandise, and are served by the Portuguese, Venetians, and Armenians with all the rarities of Europe."

Of the Persian envoy he says: "I caused his reception to be diligently observed, and found he was not favored above me at any point, but much less in several particulars."

It is worth while to add that when the Persian ambassador took his leave, he presented the king with other thirty horses, and received in return three thousand crowns.

The king removed to a camp a few miles from his palace, and at one of his audiences the English envoy had a glimpse of "his two principal wives," one of whom must have been Nur-Mahal. "They were indifferently white, with black hair smoothed up; but if there had been no other light, their diamonds and pearls had sufficed to show them. When I looked up they retired, and were so merry that I supposed they laughed at me." "Then the king came down the stairs with such an acclamation of health to the king as would have outroared cannon. Then one of his servants came, and girt on the king's sword, and hung on his buckler set all over with diamonds and rubies, the belts being of gold, suitable. On his head he wore a rich turban with a plume of heron's feathers, not many, but long. On one side of his turban hung a ruby unset, as big as a walnut; on the other side a diamond as large; in the middle an emerald like a heart, much bigger. His staff was wound about with a chain of great pearls, rubies, and diamonds, drilled. About his neck he wore a chain of most excellent pearls, the largest I ever saw. Above his elbows armlets set with diamonds, and on his wrist three rows of various sorts; his hands bare, but on almost every finger a ring."

The king and the queen, Nur-Mahal, rode in coaches made after the pattern of an English carriage which Sir Thomas Roe had brought out as a present. They had not been willing to use so plain an affair as the original one, but had had others made on the same pattern, only covered with gold and gems, somewhat to his discomfiture. In Jahangir's *Memoirs* no reference is made to the mission from England, except a bare mention of these carriages.

So they proceeded to the camp, which was a great wonder, having been set up and finished in four hours, yet it was not less than twenty English miles in compass. "The vale showed like a beautiful city, for the baggage made no confusion. I was ill provided with carriage, and ashamed of my equipage; for five years' allowance would not have provided me with an indifferent suit answerable to the others, so I returned to my poor house."

"You may add to all this," says another authority, "that the Grand Mogul keeps nigh him two or three thousand brave horses, to be always ready upon occasion ; as also eight or nine hundred elephants, and a vast number of mules, horses, and porters to carry all the great tents and their cabinets, to carry his wives, kitchens, household stuff, Ganges water, and all the other necessaries for the field which he hath always about him, as if he were at home."

The envoy was now obliged to follow the court in its migrations, finding transportation and food as best he might. He took up his lodgings in tents, or sometimes on the abandoned castles of Rajput rajahs, so beautiful "that a banished Englishman might be content to live there." He learns the intrigues of the court, and promises to tell a tale "which will discover a noble prince, an excellent wife, a faithful counsellor, a crafty step-mother, an ambitious son, a cunning favorite, all reconciled by a patient king, whose heart was not understood by any of all those." But I cannot find that he re deems his promise. He sees this patient king embrace a dirty, ragged dervish after conversing with him familiarly for an hour, which left him "in admiration to see such virtue in a heathen prince, which I mention in emulation and sorrow; wishing either that our Christian princes had this devotion, or that this zeal were guided by a true light of the gospel."

"Laws these people have none written. The king's judgment binds; who sits and gives judgment with much patience, both in civil and criminal causes, where sometimes he sees execution done by his elephants, with too much delight in blood. His governors of provinces rule by his commissions authorizing them, and take life and goods at pleasure."

"In revenue the king doubtless exceeds either Turk or Persian; the sums I dare not name; but the reason. All the land is his; no man has a foot. He maintains all that are not mechanics, by revenues bestowed on them. Favor is got by frequent presents rich and rare. The Mogul is heir to all that die. He takes all their money, only leaving the widow and daughter what he pleases. To the sons of those that die worth two or three millions, he gives some small lordship to begin the world anew. He is of countenance cheerful, not proud by nature, but only by habit and custom, for at night he is very affable and full of gentle conversation."

One of these evening conversations is more minutely described: "The good king fell to dispute of the laws of Moses, Jesus, and Mahomet, and in drink was so kind, that he turned to me and said: I am a king; you shall be welcome. Christians, Moors, Jews, he meddled not with their faith; they came all in love, and he would protect them from wrong; they lived under his safety, and none should oppress them; and this often repeated, but in extreme drunkenness, he fell to weeping and to divers passions, and so kept us till midnight."

With this we leave Sir Thomas with regret, so many of his own adventures being untouched upon.

"The Jesuits have a church at Agra," says Bernier, "and a building which they call a college, where they privately instruct the children of (some) thirty Christian families, collected I know not how in Agra, and induced to settle there by the kind and charitable aid which they receive from the Jesuits. This religious order was invited hither by Akbar, and that prince not only gave them an annual income for their maintenance, but permitted them to build churches in Agra and Lahore. The Jesuits found a still warmer patron in Jahangir, but they were sorely oppressed by Shah Jahan. That monarch deprived them of their pension, and destroyed the church at Lahore and the greater part of that at Agra." *

Jahangir's attitude towards religion is well set forth in the following story, which may not be true, but which is *ben trovato.* The Muslim doctors had admonished him against

* His empress, Mumtaz-i-Mahal, was, for some unknown reason, especially unfriendly to Christians.

the use of forbidden meats, etc.; Jahangir, becoming impatient, inquired in what religion the use of every kind of meat and drink was permitted. The reply was, in the Christian religion alone. "We must, then," said the emperor, "all turn Christians."

Professor Blochmann (*Ain-i-Akbari*, pp. 310, 477, 619) has collected a list of twenty-four of Jahangir's wives, and there easily may have been more. Their number may account for an amusing instance of the emperor's easy-going fashions. In his *Memoirs*, Jahangir says that Prince Parwiz, his child, is the son of Zain Kokah's daughter, whom he married in the forty-first year of Akbar's reign. There is no doubt whatever that Parwiz was born in the thirty-fourth year, long before Jahangir had seen the daughter of Zain. Hence it follows, apparently, that Jahangir had forgotten to which one of his many wives he was indebted for his second son.

The acts of Jahangir are given at length in his own *Memoirs* and in some of the writings of the native historians. In the following chapter of this book the history of the last years of his reign is recited. But it is not the history which is of special interest to Europeans, and still less to Americans. Our desire is to comprehend the character of this powerful and autocratic ruler, as we understand that of Louis XIV of France from the *Memoirs of Saint-Simon*. The native historians are but poor substitutes for the literary duke who has written the annals of the reign of the Very Christian King. And Jahangir's *Memoirs* are seldom worth quoting, and give but a slight picture of his personality. I append a few extracts from various sources which have a sort of value, and reserve the more important for the next chapter, which treats of the reign of the emperor's wife, who, after all, was the real ruler of the state for many years.

We read in the *Memoirs* of Jahangir: "One night I turned the discourse of my courtiers on the chase, and told them how fond of it I formerly was. At the same time it occurred to my mind whether all the animals and birds I had killed could not be calculated." The result was that from his twelfth to his fiftieth year he had killed 17,168 animals and birds with his own hand, "and the following is an account of them in detail."

* * * * * * *

Of these 86 were tigers, 90 wild boars, 1,372 deer, 13,964 birds, etc.

Two young nobles of the city were very dissipated, "lived in great pomp, and did not care for the emperor." They amused themselves by passing the palace in pleasure-boats, noisily, though they had often been warned. Jahangir gave a hint to one of his officers, and the young men were incontinently assassinated, and the emperor's peace was disturbed no more. Jahangir was fond of cruel and unusual punishments. He revived the barbarous impalements and flayings alive which had been almost forgotten. He was ingenious, too. A number of Amirs had disgraced the imperial cause by a defeat. He caused the portrait of each Amir to be painted in miniature, and, taking the portraits in hand, one by one, he showered abuse on each Amir before the assembled courtiers. In another instance, the emperor caused the offenders' heads to be shaved and women's veils to be thrown over their faces. Thus arrayed they were paraded through the city on donkeys, seated so as to face the donkeys' tails. Sewing the eyelids together was a favored mode of punishment, as also fastening the culprit inside the skin of a newly-killed animal. As the skin dried the victim perished.

"With the object of acquiring information about the history of Kabul, I used to read Babar's *Memoirs*, which all, except four parts, was written with his own hand. To complete the work, I copied those parts myself, and at the end I added some paragraphs in the Turki language to show that they were written by me. Though I was brought up in Hindustan, yet I am not deficient in reading and writing Turki."

Here is a specimen of the religious debates of which he was so fond. "One day I observed to some learned Hindus, that if the foundation of their religion rested on their belief in the ten incarnate gods, it was entirely absurd, because in such a case it became necessary to admit that the Almighty, who is infinite, must possess a definite breadth, length, and depth." "After a long discourse they admitted that there was a God who had no corporeal form and of whom they had no definite notion" (which appears to have agreed with Jahangir's own ideas). They had represented him by these ten figures so as to raise their minds up to him. "I then told them they could not attain that end by this means." Vishnu and his ten (nine) incarnations seem to be referred to here at first, and the Great First Cause at last; but the king is more practical and positive than explicit.

Jahangir was fond—too fond—of the poet Urfi, a man of real talent. These verses are his:

Cling to the hem of a heart which saddens at the plaintive voice of the nightingale; for that heart knows something.

The more I exert myself, the more I come into trouble; if I am calm, the ocean's centre is at the shore.

Not a grain shall be taken of that which thou hast reaped, but a harvest shall be demanded of that which thou hast not sown.

The emperor sets down, in his *Memoirs*, that certain tribes "associate and intermarry with Hindus, giving and taking daughters. As for taking," he says, "it does not so much matter; but as for giving their own daughters —heaven protect us!"

Here is one of the king's experiments— the trivial fooling of a muddled brain. "As it has been several times asserted that laughter arises from eating saffron, his majesty determined on making a trial of its effects, and, therefore, sent for a condemned criminal and made him eat (a large quantity) in his presence. It did not occasion any change in him. On the next day he gave him double the quantity, but it did not even cause him to smile, much less to laugh." The royal experimenter neglected an important element. He should first have *pardoned* his criminal!

Jahangir describes, in his *Memoirs*, one of the classic feats of Indian jugglery: "They produced a chain, fifty cubits in length, and threw one end of it towards the sky, where it remained as if fastened to something. A dog was brought, and immediately ran up the chain and disappeared in the air. In the same manner a hog, a panther, a lion, and a tiger were successively sent up, and all equally disappeared. At last they took down the chain and put it into a bag, no one discovering in what way the different animals were made to vanish." Similar jugglers' tricks were shown to Ibn Batuta, the Arab traveller, in 1348. The Kazi, who sat next to him, made a skeptical comment on the whole performance. "Wallah!" said he, "it is my opinion there has been neither going up nor coming down, neither marring nor mending; 'tis all hocus-pocus." The emperor is a capital witness. As this probably occurred in the daytime, he was, in all likelihood, sober. One could not ask for better evidence for this famous trick, which has been described by others also. If Indian jugglers can hypnotize an entire audience, and if they can then *suggest* to each member of it that he sees what is desired, and if every individual can be forced to recollect all the details of the performance, the trick is explicable. Otherwise, we must share Jahangir's bewilderment.*

In the sixth year of his reign (A.H. 1020), Jahangir coined his famous gold *mohur.* On one face is a portrait of the emperor in the act of raising a wine-cup to his lips; on the other is the sun in the constellation of Leo. The inscription on the coin is in Persian. Perhaps no more extraordinary coin was ever minted. The emperor broke with all traditions. The Muhammadans—at least, of the Sunni sect—did not permit the making of statues and effigies. Wine was abhorred of all good Muslims, and on this coin it was celebrated by the head of the state, who was also the head of the church. It was as if the Pope should strike a medal defiling the cross and denying the Holy Ghost.

---

* Since the foregoing was written I have noticed that Mr. Andrew Lang (*Contemporary Review* for September, 1893) seems to regard the explanation by hypnotic illusion as, at least, plausible; and Mr. Frank Stockton has adopted it, out and out, in his tale of *The Magic Egg* (*The Century* for June, 1894).

It is not strictly correct to say that Jahangir was the head of the orthodox church. The successor of Muhammad is that person who has the custody of the relics of the prophet (his cloak, teeth,

The face is interesting, and it is probably an unflattered likeness, as it resembles portraits of Jahangir which are accepted as authentic. The jaw is heavy, the nose long, and broad at the base, and the expression astute and sly. In the same year another coin was minted, where the wine-cup is exchanged for a book (which can only be the Kuran), and on which the expression of the emperor's face is entirely changed. His attitude is one of dignity; his face is softened and refined; he is no longer the violator, but the protector, of the law.

It has been surmised that the first coin gave such occasion of scandal (as well it might) that the second was struck to take its place. This may be so, but it then becomes difficult to explain why another coin was minted in the year A.H. 1023, three years later, in which the wine-cup again appears. The sun on these coins serves to recall the fact that the emperor was born on a Sunday.

beard, etc.), and who rules the sacred cities of Mecca and Medina. These titles belong to the Sultan of Constantinople (the Khalife = successor). But in India the orthodox doctors of the law had declared the emperor to be the head of the church.

Jahangir also caused a silver medal to be struck soon after his father's death, which bears the effigy of Akbar. The face has only a moustache, and not the beard of the orthodox Muslim. Yet the obverse of the medal bears the profession of faith : *There is no God but God; Muhammad is the Apostle of God.*

With this we may leave this nest of tyrants. The atmosphere in which they lived is foreign to us, and their actions seem wild and barbarous to us Western folk who live our orderly lives between well-drawn lines which we do not overstep. "Custom makes cowards of us all," and habit makes us unreflecting. These Oriental despots were no more savage or vindictive or careless than the Cæsars ; and we have long ago accepted them as part of our ancestry.

It is clear that Sir Thomas Roe, a model Briton, was continually and unconsciously comparing the Emperor Jahangir with his own English king, not always to the advantage of the latter. Even to us, who have crossed the seas and the centuries, there is something not totally unfamiliar in this Oriental nature freely displayed under strange and outlandish conditions.

Coelum, non animum mutant, qui trans mare currunt.

NOTE.—The description of Jahangir's coins on pages 232 *et seq.* was written after consulting the older authorities (Marsden, etc.), the only ones then available to me. It is not strictly correct in several respects. Those interested should refer to Dr. R. S. Poole's *Coins of the Moghul Emperors*, London, 1892, pages lxxx, 62, etc., where plates of these coins are given.

CHAPTER VI

NUR-MAHAL (THE LIGHT OF THE PALACE), EMPRESS OF HINDUSTAN (A.D. 1611–1627)

IN the history of the reigns of the Great Moguls, the women of the royal house seldom appear, except in the character of devoted or intriguing wives and mothers, whose words are never heard on this side of the curtain which shuts them away from the world. The fierce light which beats upon the throne penetrates the harem only to make a twilight of mystery and intrigue. There is one great and striking exception in the person of the Empress Nur-Mahal, whose reign was nearly contemporaneous with that of King James I. of England, the successor of Elizabeth, and who may fairly be compared with that great English queen.

We are more or less familiar in the Western world with the power of women in government. But our Western heroines—Frede-

NUR-MAHAL

gonde, Joan of Arc, Madame de Stael—have been personages who could be seen and heard. The Indian queen, after the time of Babar, was confined to the harem, and could be seen only by her nearest relations, and could be heard only from behind the curtain. I have met but two works which give a realizing sense of the power of Oriental women; namely, the brilliant novel of Kipling and Balestier, *The Naulakha* (1892), and the *Memoirs* of a certain *wazir*, one Nizamu-l-Mulk Tusi (A.D. 1092), some eight hundred years earlier. The *wazir's* whole history is interesting. His accounts of the power of female intrigue are pathetic. "Now, from what I have said, the disadvantages of the ladies of the royal household being against us (*wazirs*) may be learned. But the advantages of their being in our favor are equally numerous," as he goes on to show by a story too long to relate. He quotes the words of a powerful minister who resigned his office and went to govern a remote province, as an example. "What made him prefer it to a rank in which he exercised influence over the whole kingdom?" "O Imam!" the ex-minister says, "I have not told this secret even to my sons, but I will not conceal the truth from you. I have resigned that power on account of Jamila Kandahari (one of the queen's ladies). For years I had the management of all the government in my hands, and she thwarted me in everything. For this reason there was darkness before my eyes, and I could find no remedy against the evil. Now I have sought retirement, and have procured release from all such troubles. If Allah pleases, I shall escape her machinations in this distant province."

The Emperor Jahangir had succeeded Akbar in the year 1605. In the thirty-first year of Akbar's reign he had rebelled against his father, and had set up a separate government in the Penjab and appropriated the revenue (thirty lacs of rupees) to his own use. To remove his chief enemy at court, he had basely murdered his father's prime minister and attached friend, the learned Abul-fazl, and had embittered the last days of his great sire by violent, cruel, and rebellious acts. "About the close of my father's reign Abul-fazl was wearing on his plausible exterior the jewel of probity, which he sold to my father at a high price. He was not my friend. His bearing fully convinced me that if he were allowed to arrive at court he would do everything in his power to excite the indignation of my father against me. Under this apprehension I invited Nar Singh to annihilate Abul-fazl on his journey, promising him favors. God aided the enterprise; Abul-faẓl's followers were put to flight, and he himself murdered. His head was sent to me at Allahabad." Such is Jahangir's own account.

Akbar's death is ascribed to his vexation at a disgraceful and public quarrel between Jahangir and his son Khosrou about the merits of their respective elephants at a fight of animals.

He was remorseless, even vindictive, in the punishment of crimes against the state—that is, against himself—and this seems in a large measure to have been a matter of settled policy on his part. Jahangir had an intimate horror of everything that tended to disturb the indifferent thoughtlessness of his self-indulgent and careless life. In the early portion of his reign he was obliged to stamp out a rebellion fomented by his son Khosrou. His own words are : "I entered the castle at Lahore, and took my seat in the royal pavilion built by my father, and I directed that a number of sharp stakes should be set up, upon which thrones of misfortune and despair I caused the seven hundred traitors to be impaled alive. Than this there cannot be," he goes on, "a more excruciating punishment, for the culprits die in lingering torture."

His son was finally captured, paraded between the lines of impaled victims, and then imprisoned. He spent the time in tears and groans for his past misconduct, and no doubt in deadly fear for his own life. He doubtless recalled his father's express declaration that "Sovereignty does not regard the relation of father and son ; and it is said a king should deem no one his relation." Kingship knows no kinship.

Jahangir always evinced "too much delight in blood," and his violence was often due to intoxication by wine or opium. "From that time I took to wine drinking," he says, "and from day to day took more and more, until it had no effect upon me, and I resorted to drinking spirits. In the course of nine years I got up to twenty cups of spirit, fourteen of which I drank in the day, and six at night." Finally, he was warned to stop by a faithful (and courageous) physician. "His advice was good, and life was dear; and for fifteen years I have kept to six cups, neither more nor less." Opium took the place of the abandoned cups. Two of his brothers died from drunkenness.

In spite of this dark picture, there are many excellent, even admirable, traits in his character. He was self-indulgent and capricious, rather than deliberately vicious. The very first act of his reign was to set up the "chain of justice" in his palace at Agra—a golden chain sixty feet long, reaching from the ground to his chamber. On this chain were sixty golden bells, and a suitor for justice could call the emperor's attention to his claim without the intervention of any person.*

His *Memoirs*, from which I have already quoted, are addressed to his sons and disciples, and begin thus:

"First, let them know that the world is not eternal, and that the less care they have for it the better. Act towards your inferiors as you wish that your superiors should act towards you." It is clear that the Jesuits of Goa had left their mark; and indeed he

---

* The idea was not original. The drums of Humayun were established for the same end. Sultan Shamsu-d-din Altamsh, (A.D. 1211) at Delhi, "made an order that any man who suffered from injustice should wear colored clothes Now all the inhabitants of India wear white clothes, so that whenever he rode abroad and saw any one in a colored dress he inquired into his grievance, and took means to render him justice. But he was not satisfied (even) with this plan, and said, 'Some men suffer injustice in the night, and I wish to give them redress.' So he placed at the door of his palace two marble lions on two pedestals. These lions had iron chains round their necks from which hung great bells. The victim of injustice came at night and rung the bell, and when the Sultan heard it he inquired into the case and gave satisfaction to the complainant."

was wonderfully tolerant of all religions, although he did not (openly) go so far in this direction as his father. "No king was ever more generous and kind to beggars" or to religious mendicants—*fakirs*—or more anxious for new light from holy men.

Jahangir had been born in the house of a famous Muslim saint, and was at first called by his name (Selim).

"A famous place of worship is in this neighborhood," he says, "and I went to see it in the possible chance of meeting some *fakir* from whose society I might derive advantage; but such a man is as rare as the philosopher's stone, and all that I saw was a small fraternity without any knowledge of God, the sight of whom filled my heart with nothing but regret."

He encouraged all sorts of learning at his court, and was lavish in distribution of alms from his audience window every week (on Sundays). He was fond of architecture and art, and devoted to the beauties of natural scenery and flowers, even childishly so. On his way to Kashmir the army marched along a river bed, "and the oleander bushes were in full bloom, and of exquisite color, like peach-blossoms. I ordered my attendants to bind bunches of the flowers in their turbans, and I thus devised a beautiful garden." At another camp the flowers were so beautiful that "it was a sight such that it was impossible to take one's eyes off it." He goes on, "As the air was very charming (and the flowers beautiful), I indulged myself in drinking wine. In short, I enjoyed myself amazingly on this march."

It is surprising to us to meet this appreciation of nature in the Mogul character, but it is a genuine quality. Chengiz-Khan, that bloodthirsty savage, in describing a spot in Tartary, says, "It is a beautiful grazing ground for roebucks, and a charming resting place for an old man"—as he then was. To the Moguls, nature was beautiful, but it was something outside of themselves; the Greeks felt themselves a part of it.

Jahangir goes on to say, "Kashmir is a delightful country in the seasons of autumn and of spring. I visited it and found it even more charming than I had anticipated. There is no other place in the world where saffron is so abundantly cultivated. The fields of saffron are sometimes two miles in length, and they look very beautiful at a distance. It has such a strong smell that people get a headache from it. I asked the Kashmirians whether it had any such effect upon them, and was surprised by their reply, which was, that they did not even know what headache was." "The surface of the land is so covered with green that it requires no carpet to be spread upon it." The place was full of wonders, and they showed the sceptical king a fountain of "unfathomable depth." He ordered it sounded by a stone and a rope, and the depth turned out to be nine feet.

He was a mighty hunter,* brave, fond of manly sports, devoted and affectionate to his friends, always providing that their actions did not affect the safety or welfare of the state, and again *l'état c'était lui;* and cruel

---

* He had killed eighty-six tigers with his own hand, and ninety wild boars.

and vindictive in the contrary case. He was deeply attached to his first wife, the daughter of the Rajah Bhagwan Das of Amber, and the mother of his rebellious son Khosroü. "How can I describe her excellence and good nature? Her affection for me was such that she would have given a thousand sons as a ransom for one hair of mine. She was my first bride, and I was married to her in youth. Her death had such an effect upon me that I did not care to live. For four days and nights I did not care to eat or drink." It is recorded, also, and it is very likely to be true, that after Nur-Mahal had become his empress he declared, "Before I married her, I never knew the real meaning of marriage." The Persian woman was made of different clay from the daughters of the Rajput princes.

These extracts from his own sayings give a picture of the capricious despot who succeeded to the just and benevolent Akbar.

Professor Dowson, the editor of Elliott's *History of India as told by its own Histo-*

rians, has made a calm estimate of Jahangir's character.

"The autobiography proves Jahangir to have been a man of no common ability. He records his weaknesses and confesses his faults with candor, and a perusal of this work alone would leave a favorable impression of his character and talents. He was fond of jewels, of flowers, of architecture, a lover of nature, a mighty hunter. He seems to have been just, and even generous, when he was sober; but even as prince-royal he was noted for his ruthless punishments when he was in his cups."

Such was the king who received the sovereignty of India from the dying Akbar, and who then "began to win the hearts of all the people and to rearrange the withered world." While he was yet crown-prince, he had seen in the women's apartments a young girl of remarkable beauty for whom he formed a passionate attachment. This was Mihrunnisa, afterwards Nur-Mahal. Her mother found means to lay the case before Akbar, who remonstrated with his son, and who, the better to guard against a *mésalliance*, married the girl to one of his own officers, Shir-Afghan-Khan, on whom he bestowed a government in distant Bengal. The newly wedded pair departed to their government, and the prince was duly married to the grand-daughter of a great rajah, and became a power in the state, warring and making war, sometimes for his father, oftener on his own account in rebellion.

The grandfather of Nur-Mahal had been *wazir* to the governor of Khorassan. In consequence of adverse circumstances his son Mirza Ghiyas Beg set out for Hindustan to retrieve his fortunes. His caravan was plundered, and he was reduced to abject poverty. When he reached Kandahar, in the year 1585, his wife was delivered of a girl child, Mihrunnisa—the sun of women—afterwards called Nur-Mahal. So desperate had their condition become that the infant was exposed on the highway to perish. One of the chief merchants of the caravan, seeing the beauty of the child, and moved by pity, took her up and resolved to educate her as his own daughter. His first care was to seek for a nurse, and the only available nurse in the party was, naturally, the child's mother. The relation thus strangely brought about was the turning point in their career. When they reached the city of Fathpur, Ghiyas Beg was presented to the Emperor Akbar, and in a short time he was raised to the office of superintendent of the household, and the fortunes of the family were made.

"He was considered exceedingly clever and skilful both in writing and in transacting business. He had studied the old poetry, and had a nice appreciation of the meaning of words, and his handwriting was bold and elegant"—accomplishments which would commend him to the emperor. "His leisure moments were devoted to the study of poetry and style; and his generosity and beneficence to the poor were such that no one ever turned disappointed from his door." He was on the high road to prosperity, and improved his opportunities to the full. "In the taking of bribes he certainly was most uncompromising and fearless"! His wife, too, was a woman of note. Jahangir relates that she invented *attar of roses*.* "She conceived the idea of collecting the oil which rises to the surface when rose-water is heated, and the oil was found to be a powerful perfume." The daughter, also, was unusually accomplished in the arts of painting and fine needlework, it is said, and she wrote a few Persian poems also. Their son Asaf-Khan rose to be prime minister under the succeeding reign, and no subject of an Indian king ever enjoyed a like prosperity. In 1641 he died, and was buried near the tomb of the Emperor Jahangir, his master. His palace in Lahore had cost a million dollars, and the jewels, plate, and money which he left were valued at over twelve millions.. His daughter Arjamand (afterwards Mumtaz-i-Mahal) married the Prince Khurram (afterwards Shah Jahan).

In the meantime Jahangir's first wife had died, and he had ascended the throne. In

---

* *Antar*, an Arab novel of the eighth century, mentions *attar of roses*, however.

the first year of his reign he sent his foster-brother Kutbu-d-Din to Bengal as viceroy, and charged him with a mission to procure the divorce of Nur-Mahal and to send her to him. Details regarding these negotiations are not known, but it is certain that they were received with anger by Shir-Afghan, her husband; and probably Nur-Mahal never heard of them at all. At all events, she appears to have been sincerely attached to her first husband.

In the second year of the reign, the viceroy, having received commands to send Shir-Afghan to court, made an official visit to his government. The men of the viceroy crowded around Shir-Afghan, who had only two attendants, and who asked "quietly" what this kind of proceeding meant. The viceroy ordered his men to stand apart, and engaged in a conversation in which, no doubt, the desires of the emperor were again declared, and a promise of immunity given in case the husband should prove docile and complaisant. However this may be, the outraged noble immediately killed the viceroy with a dagger which he had concealed, and was himself at once cut to pieces by the viceroy's troops.*

The future empress was sent to Agra, and was attached to the suite of the empress dowager Jahangir was sorely distressed by the death of his foster-brother in such a cause, and Nur-Mahal seems to have repulsed his offer of marriage with disgust, and to have made the emperor forget her. "She remained some time without notice." This "some time" must have been about four years, for it was not until the sixth year (A.D. 1611) of the reign that "the days of misfortune drew to a close, and the stars of her

* One of the historians relates the end of Shir-Afghan differently. He says that Shir was not killed outright (which is unlikely), but managed to drag himself to the door of his house, intending to kill his wife rather than to let her fall into Jahangir's hands. Nur-Mahal's mother would not let him enter, and declared to him that his wife had already committed suicide by throwing herself into a well. "Having heard the sad news, Shir-Afghan went to the heavenly mansions." The Muslim comment on such stories is appropriate here—Allah knows if this be true. Jahangir remarks of Shir-Afghan's death in his *Memoirs* that he hopes "the black-faced wretch will forever remain in hell," which seems cruel and in keeping with his character.

good fortune commenced to shine, and to wake as it were from a deep sleep." "The bride's chamber was prepared, the bride was decorated, and desire began to arise. Hope was happy. A key was found for clcsed doors, a restorative for broken hearts; and on a certain New Year's festival she (again) attracted the love and affection of the king." Thus lamely does the native chronicler recite the history. "She was soon made the favorite wife of his majesty. She received at first the title of Nur-Mahal (*the light of the palace*), and after some days that of Nur-Jahan-Begam (*the queen, the light of the world*)."

Up to this time she had led the usual life of an Oriental lady of rank, hidden from the eyes of men, and having only an occult influence upon the petty affairs of a small government. At one step she became the chief personage in India. "All her relatives were elevated to the highest offices of the state. Her father became prime minister, and the king and his relatives were thus deprived of all power. Nur-Mahal managed the whole affairs of the realm, and honors of every description were at her disposal, and nothing was wanting to make her an absolute monarch, except reading the *Khutba* * in her name." The Persian child who had been abandoned in the desert had become the veritable ruler of all India. She was now twenty-six years old. "Day by day," says another historian, "her influence and dignity increased. No grant of land was bestowed upon any woman, except under her seal. She was granted the rights of sovereignty. She would sit in the balcony of her palace while the nobles would present themselves (as to a king) and listen to her dictates. Coin was struck in her name with this superscription:

> *By order of King Jahangir, gold has a hundred splendors added to it by receiving the impression of the name of Nur-Jahan the queen.*

"She signed all *farmans* jointly with the king. At last her authority reached such a pitch that the king was such only in name.

* The official prayers.

"She commands and governs at this day in the king's harem with supreme authority, having cunningly removed out of the harem, either by marriage or other handsome ways, all the other women who might give her any jealousy; and having also in the court made many alterations by deposing and displacing almost all the old captains and officers, and by advancing to dignities other new ones of her own creatures, and particularly those of her blood and alliance."

By this time the affairs of the kingdom were in excellent shape, and the self-indulgent Jahangir laughed and said that he had bestowed the government on the most competent. As for himself, he asked only wine and meat. When he was ill he dismissed the physicians (who were indeed of small account), and depended only on the empress, "whose sense and experience" exceeded theirs. "It is impossible to describe the beauty and wisdom of the queen; in any matter that was presented to her, if a difficulty arose she immediately solved it." She was benevolent to all, protecting some from tyranny, and portioning penniless orphans. "She won golden opinions from all people." The greatest of all her benefits was in modifying the tyrannical and capricious conduct of the emperor, and in introducing by her own intelligence and good taste, powerfully aided in the wise conduct of state affairs by her father, now *wazir*, something like a steady policy. The affairs of the kingdom were prosperous; justice of a sort was easily attainable; the court was magnificent by her taste; liberal through Jahangir's good nature and her tact. The praise which has been bestowed on another Indian Sultana,* is justly her due. "She was endowed with every princely virtue, and those who scrutinize her actions most severely will find in her no fault but that she was a woman."

Jahangir had four sons; Khosrou, the eldest, had been in open rebellion and was in disgrace. His father had always disliked him, but the people attributed his exclusion from the court to the influence of Asaf-Khan and the empress. He died suddenly

* Rezia Begum, *circa* A.D. 1240.

"of a colic," while in the custody of his brother Shah Jahan, at a time when the emperor was ill; and his death was attributed (very likely falsely) to his keeper. Prince Parwiz, the second son, was a brave and dissipated soldier, and little more. Shah Jahan had shown very high military talents, and had obtained great successes. He had married a niece of Nur-Mahal's,* and was sustained at court (at this time) by her powerful influence; and for this reason, and because of his marked talent for government, he was the favorite of his father. To all people, even to the greatest nobles, he was cold and haughty. "He was flattered by some, envied by others, loved by none."

The youngest son of Jahangir was Prince Shahriyar, who was affianced to the daughter who was born to Nur-Mahal of her alliance with the unfortunate Shir-Afghan-Khan. Up to the time of their engagement, Nur-Mahal

* His favorite wife was Arjamand, better known as Mumtaz-i-Mahal (the exalted of the palace), the daughter of Asaf-Khan; the niece consequently of Nur-Mahal. She was born in 1590, and at her death, in 1630, she was buried in the Taj-Mahal; she bore many sons and daughters to Shah Jahan.

had been a strong partisan of Shah Jahan. But his success had made him overbearing, and the empress began to realize that she could never mould him to her purposes. Her influence was thus transferred to the cause of Shahriyar, where her interest lay. At this very juncture the father of Nur-Mahal died, which was all the more unfortunate, as the contentions of the princes and of their various partisans among the high nobles began to be troublesome. Her brother Azaf-Khan, who became prime minister in his father's stead, was far too weak to master events, which went from ill to worse. The power of Shah Jahan grew daily, and if it were to be curbed at all, it must be done at once. Accordingly Nur-Mahal cast about for a general who should be devoted to her cause, to lead the imperial armies. Her eye fell upon Mahabet-Khan, one of the great nobles. Mahabet-Khan was a *saiyid*, a descendant of the Prophet, of high family. His lineage is to be traced (if we are to believe one of his family) "directly to the prophet Moses." Mahabet-

Khan in his youth entered the service of Jahangir, then crown-prince, and became a prime favorite with him by (treacherously) murdering a Hindu rajah who stood in the prince's way. Sir Thomas Roe calls him, however, a noble and generous man, well beloved by all men; and he had risen to be the most eminent of all the nobles. This general, accompanied for a time by the emperor, and later by Prince Parwiz, drove Shah Jahan away from the vicinity of Agra and into the Deccan; and so thorough was Shah Jahan's defeat that Jahangir felt at liberty to go, for two successive summers, to Kashmir.

The emperor had not been a very loyal and docile son to Akbar, and had given his father much pain and anxiety by his open opposition. All this was returned to him ten-fold by the conduct of his own son Shah Jahan. Jahangir does not mention him by name in parts of his *Memoirs*, but calls him "the wretch." "Whenever the word 'wretch' occurs here, it is my son who is referred to." "The pen cannot describe what I have done for him, nor the anxiety and grief which oppress me during the (military) marches which I am obliged to make in pursuit of him who is no longer my son."

The close connection of Mahabet-Khan with Prince Parwiz led to the fear that he would endeavor to place this prince upon the throne, and it was resolved to ruin him. Accordingly Asaf-Khan recalled him to the court, "to bring him to disgrace, and to deprive him of honor, property, and life. But he had cleverly seen through Asaf-Khan's designs, and had brought with him four or five thousand Rajput warriors united in one cause." He also brought with him the war-elephants. "The abiding place of the emperor was on the bank of the River Behat," where a bridge had been built. Mahabet-Khan with his army came to the court at this bridge. "Asaf-Khan, notwithstanding the presence of so brave and daring an enemy, was so heedless of the emperor's safety, that he left him on that side of the river with the children and women. He sent over also the baggage, the treasure, the arms, etc., even to the very domestics. Mahabet-Khan perceived that his life and honor were at stake, and that he had not a single friend at court." He resolved on a bold stroke. With about two hundred Rajputs he suddenly appeared at the chief entrance to the royal tents. Let us quote the account of one of the royal household who was an eye-witness. "Mahabet-Khan rode to the door of the state room and alighted. I then went forward, and in my simplicity exclaimed, 'This presumption and temerity exceeds all bounds. If you will wait a moment, I will go in and make a report. He did not trouble himself to answer." "His attendants tore down a board partition. The emperor came out from behind it, and seated himself. The Khan approached him respectfully, and said, 'I have assured myself that escape from the hatred of Asaf-Khan is impossible, and that I shall be put to death in shame. I have therefore boldly and presumptuously thrown myself on your Majesty's protection. If I deserve death or punishment, give the order, that I may suffer it in your presence.' "

But it was for the Khan to make terms, for his troops flocked in, and the emperor was a prisoner without a blow. Jahangir was wild with rage, but almost instantly controlled himself, and began that course of dissimulation which led to his release in the end. He consented to ride out before the troops on an elephant to the hunting-ground, and was then forced to go to the Khan's quarters. All this time Mahabet-Khan had taken no thought of Nur-Mahal, and he determined to make her a prisoner also. "But, as it happened, Nur-Mahal, thinking that his Majesty had gone out hunting, took the opportunity to pass over the river to pay a visit to her brother Asaf-Khan." Mahabet-Khan bitterly repented of the blunder he had made in not securing her at once, and he proceeded with the emperor to the house of Prince Shahriyar, where they spent the night.

"After Nur-Mahal had crossed the river,

she summoned all the chief nobles, and addressed them in reproachful terms. 'This,' she said, 'has happened through your neglect and stupid arrangements.* What never entered into the imagination of any one has come to pass, and now you stand stricken with shame for your conduct. You must do your best to repair this evil.'"

The bridge had been destroyed, and the nobles resolved to pass the river at a ford, and to give battle to the rebel.

The ford was a bad one, and everything was in confusion. "I (says the officer whose account is quoted above) had crossed one branch of the river, and was standing on the brink of the other, watching the working of destiny. At this time an officer of the empress came and said, 'The Begam wants to know if *this* is a time for delay and irresolution. Strike boldly forward.'" The empress herself was in the press, mounted on an elephant, and

---

* It is impossible not to suspect treachery on the part of Asaf-Khan. Though Nur-Mahal was his sister, his daughter was the wife of Shah Jahan.

nearly reached the opposite shore, which was defended by swarms of Rajputs. Her attendant in the howdah was wounded, and the empress pulled out the arrow and was covered with the blood. This could not affright her, for she was a brave and skilful hunter who had killed tigers with a single shot.* However, she was at last forced to turn back, and the army was defeated. Asaf-Khan fled to his fort, which was invested and captured, and Asaf bound himself to support the cause of Mahabet-Khan. The emperor and Nur-Mahal remained prisoners of the Khan, who gave orders in their name.

"His majesty, in his great good nature, and gentleness,† had now become reconciled

---

* In Jahangir's own *Memoirs* we read: "My huntsmen reported that there was a tiger in the neighborhood. I ordered his retreat to be surrounded. I told Nur-Jahan to fire my musket. The smell of the tiger made the elephant very restless and he would not stand still; and to take good aim from a *howdah* is a very difficult feat. Mirza Rustam, who, after me, has no equal as a marksman, has fired three or four shots from an elephant's back without effect. Nur-Jahan, however, killed this tiger with the first shot."

† Which, beyond a doubt, were assumed.

to Mahabet-Khan, and showed him great favor, so that he felt quite secure on that side. Whatever Nur-Mahal said to the emperor in private, he repeated to the Khan, and he bade him beware, for she had a design upon him. Mahabet became less watchful. Besides, he had lost some of his best soldiers in the fight. Nur-Mahal worked against him in private and public." She suggested to the emperor to order a review of the troops, and as she was an over-lord of a district near by, she mustered a formidable array of cavalry devoted to her cause.

The review was held, and Mahabet-Khan was prevailed upon to absent himself with many of his own troops, lest blood should be again shed. His weakness induced him to accede, and he left the emperor surrounded by only a portion of his Rajputs. At the review, the cavalry of the empress pressed close around this guard and overawed it, and once more the emperor was his own master—saved by his own crafty dissimulation and by the more manly energy of the empress. Mahabet-Khan received peremptory orders to march at once against Shah Jahan, and to send Asaf-Khan back to court. He hesitated to obey the latter order, "which greatly enraged the Begam," who sent him a second message which cowed him, and which was promptly obeyed. He set off on his journey with about two thousand troops, and joined his fortunes with Prince Shah Jahan, whom he had been sent to destroy.

It was at this very time that Prince Parwiz died in "a heavy sleep." His illness was attributed to excessive drinking, but, as Muhammadans say in doubtful cases, "Allah knows if this be true." Poisonings were suspected in this reign as freely as in that of Louis XIV of France, a century later. He was in the custody of his brother Shah Jahan. The twenty-second year of the reign of Jahangir had now begun. Nur-Mahal was all-powerful, but the forces of Shah Jahan were increasing. Sultan Shahriyar also became ill, and was obliged to leave Kashmir, where the emperor had gone. The emperor himself fell ill, with a return of his old disease, the asthma. He refused wine, and rapidly grew worse, and died October 28, 1627, at the age of fifty-nine years.

Shah Jahan was his designated successor, but Nur-Mahal clung to the vain idea of retaining the reins of government which she had held so long, and intrigued to cause Sultan Shahriyar to rebel. The sons of Shah Jahan were still in the female apartments with Nur-Mahal, but they "were not safe with her," and they were accordingly removed from her charge. By February, 1628, all obstacles had been removed, and on the 6th of that month Shah Jahan ascended the throne after Shahriyar had been captured and blinded.*

"Thus had he (through a sea of blood) attained the highest post and dignity of the

---

* Shahriyar was the most beautiful of all the princes. Once when he was troubled with a severe pain in his eyes, he was cured by Mukawab Khan. The emperor heard of his cure and cynically remarked, that no doubt his eyes would remain entirely well until they were put out by his brothers—as indeed came to pass. To insure a safe title to the throne, Shah Jahan felt obliged to do away with the sons of his brothers Khosrou, Parwiz, Daniel, and Morad: All these were executed and buried at Lahore, and their heads sent to Shah Jahan. His reign was not troubled by rival claimants to the throne.

Eastern world, surrounded with delights and guarded by a power, in his conceiving, unresistable." When Herbert wrote this (in 1638) the favorite Mumtaz-i-Mahal had been dead eight years, and it was rumored he had taken her daughter to wife, "incest of so high nature that that yeare his whole empire was wounded with God's arrowes of plague, pestilence, and famine, this thousand yeares before never so terrible."

Nur-Mahal's influence was now completely gone, and her name is not again heard of till her death in 1645.* She was treated with respect, and received a handsome income—ninety-four thousand dollars (two *lacs*) a year as empress-dowager. She wore no color but white after the emperor's death, abstained from all entertainments, and appeared to

* At the age of sixty years. Professor Blochmann (p. 510) says she died at Lahore in A.H. 1055 at the age of seventy-two. Keene (*Agra Guide*) has the same remark. I believe the date of her birth to have been A.D. 1585. Akbar was in the Penjab directing the campaigns against Kashmir and the Afghans during 1586 and 1587. It was at this time, I think, that the father of Nur-Mahal was presented to the emperor in the city of Fathpur. (*Native Historians*, vol. vi., p. 404.)

devote her life entirely to the memory of her husband. She is buried in a tomb at Lahore, near Jahangir.

It is almost impossible to compare the career and talents of an Asiatic and a Western ruler. The circumstances are utterly unlike, and our familiar standards fail. Bad, weak, and cruel as Jahangir was, he does not seem more despicable than James I. of England, for example, who was his contemporary. His empress was unsuccessful in her plans, where no skill or wisdom would have prevailed, while Elizabeth of England succeeded in her policy. If we think of the contemporaries of the Indian empress, we shall not find her equal. We are forced to go back to the great Elizabeth for a term of comparison even. While she lived, Nur-Mahal was the greatest personage in all Asia, if not in the whole world.

CHAPTER VII

SHAH JAHAN AND AURANGZEB, EMPERORS OF HINDUSTAN (A.D. 1628–1658 AND A.D. 1658–1707)

THE reigns of these two princes are recounted in a famous work by Monsieur Bernier, a man no less intelligent than Sir Thomas Roe. A preface to his volume gives some small account of him. "Monsieur Bernier, after he had benefited himself for many years by the converse of the famous Gassendi, and had seen him expire in his arms, succeeded him in his knowledge, and inherited his opinions and discoveries, (then) embarked for Egypt, stayed above a whole year at Cairo, and took the occasion of some Indian vessels to pass to Surat, and abode twelve years at the court of the Great Mogul. His prudent conduct made him merit the esteem of his generous master, Fazel-Khan, who since is become the first

SHAH JAHAN

minister of that great empire, to whom he taught the principal languages of Europe, after he had translated for him the whole philosophy of Gassendi from the Latin, and whose leave he could not obtain to go home till he had got for him a select number of our best European books, thereby to supply the loss he should suffer of his person. Never a traveller went from home more capable to observe, nor hath written with more knowledge, candor, and integrity."

And after this preface the history of Bernier begins by reciting his arrival at Surat in the year 1655. "I found that he who reigned there was called Shah Jahan, that is to say, king of the world. He was the tenth of those who were descended from Tamerlane, which signifieth the lame prince, who married his near kinswoman, the only daughter of the prince of the nations of Great Tartary, called Moguls, who have (thus) communicated their name to the strangers that now govern Hindustan, the country of the Indians, though those that are employed in public charges and offices, and even those that are listed in the militia, be (from) nations gathered out of all countries, most of them Persians, some Arabians, and some Turks."

"I found also at my arrival that this Shah Jahan, of above seventy years of age, had four sons and two daughters; that some years since he had made these four sons vice-kings, or governors of provinces; that it was almost a year that he was fallen into a great sickness, whence it was believed he would never recover; which had occasioned a great division among these four brothers (all laying claim to the empire), and had kindled among them a war which lasted about five years, and which I design here to describe."

We cannot follow the very intelligent narrative of Bernier of the rise of Aurangzeb, one of the four sons, to power. This is compactly set forth in the original work, which is a large book of itself. The intrigue is so close and constant that the narrative can scarcely bear condensation. It is more to my purpose to give in Bernier's own words some of the incidents of which he had personal knowledge. He was at this court in the quality of a physician under salary from one of the great lords who was, he says, "the most knowing man in Asia."

It will be necessary to name the children of the king: "The eldest of these four sons was called Dara, that is, Darius; the second was called Sultan-Sujah, that is, the valiant prince; the name of the third was Aurangzeb, which signifies the ornament of the throne; that of the fourth was Morad-Bakche, as if you should say, desire accomplished. The eldest daughter was called Begum-Saheb, that is, the mistress princess; and the youngest, Rauchenara-Begum, which is as much as bright princess, or the splendor of princesses."

Here is Bernier's penetrating estimate of the character of the members of this nest of tyrants: "Dara, the eldest son, wanted not in good qualities. He was gallant, witty, exceeding civil and liberal, but entertained so good an opinion of his person that he was intolerant of all counsel, so that even those most affectionate to him were shy of discovering secret intrigues to him. He was extremely passionate in anger and affronted even the greatest nobles. Though he was a Muhammadan in public, he was, probably, a mere heathen in private, and it is certain that he encouraged both Hindus and Jesuits. This laxness in religion was afterwards turned much against his advantage in the struggles for the throne." *

"Sultan-Sujah, the second son, was much of the humor of Dara, but he was more close and more settled, and had better conduct and dexterity."

"Aurangzeb, the third brother, had not that gallantry nor surprising presence of Dara; he appeared more serious and melancholy, and, indeed, was much more judicious, understanding the world very well. He was reserved, crafty, and exceedingly versed in dissembling; inasmuch that for a long while

* Dara's adherents were chiefly Hindus, and the prince translated the *Upanishads* from Sanscrit into Persian. Professor Max Müller makes the curious remark that Dara's Persian version was the basis of the Latin translation upon which Schopenhauer declares that his system is founded.

he made profession to be (a) *fakir*, renouncing the world, and feigning not to pretend at all to the crown, but to desire to pass his life in prayer and other devotions. In the meantime he failed not to make a party at court with dexterity, art, and secrecy. He also had the skill to maintain himself in the affection of Shah Jahan, his father."

"Morad-Bakche, the youngest of all, was the least dextrous and the least judicious. He cared for nothing but mirth and pastime, to drink, hunt and shoot; he was very civil and liberal, despised cabals, and bragged openly that he trusted only in his arm and sword."

"Concerning the two daughters, the eldest, Begum-Saheb, was very beautiful and a great wit, passionately beloved of her father. It was even rumored that he loved her to that degree as is hardly to be imagined. He had given her charge to watch over his safety and to have an eye to all that came to his table, and she knew perfectly to manage his humor, and to bend him as she pleased. She stuck entirely to Dara, and espoused cordially his part, because he had promised her that so soon as he should come to the crown he would (find a husband for her); which is almost never practiced in Indostan" (as the royal princesses were so far in rank above any subjects).

Bernier relates one of the adventures of this princess, as "they are not amours like ours, but attended with events dreadful and tragical." It appears that she received one of her lovers into her apartments, and that, as Shah Jahan was about to enter, she had nowhere to conceal him except in one of the large hot-water caldrons made to bathe in. The emperor feigned to see nothing, but after a long visit sternly commanded a fire to be built beneath the bath, and did not leave till the man was dead.

"Her sister, Rauchenara-Begum, never passed for so handsome and witty as Begum-Saheb, but she was not less cheerful, and comely enough, and hated pleasures no more than her sister; but she addicted herself wholly to Aurangzeb, and consequently declared herself an enemy to Begum-Saheb and to Dara." Mumtaz-i-Mahal, their mother, had been dead for some years, and was buried in her glorious tomb, the Taj-Mahal. She died in giving birth to the younger sister.

"So Shah Jahan, finding himself charged with these four princes, all come of age, all pretending to the crown, enemies to one another, and each of them secretly forming a party, was perplexed enough as to what was fittest for him to do." They were too powerful to be imprisoned, and he was constrained to set them over distant parts of the empire, though this course gave each of them power and an army of his own.

A trifling incident placed Aurangzeb in alliance with Emir-Jemla, *wazir* of Golconda. These two great men were not long together till they framed large designs. And, first of all, the emperor was presented with "that great diamond which is esteemed matchless.* Presents and intrigue put the two friends into the possession of new powers, and gave them new armies; and every gain to them seemed a loss to Dara, who was with his

---

* This was the *Kohinur*.

father at court. In the midst of these events Shah Jahan fell sick, and it was thought he must die.

Mighty armies were raised by Dara at Agra and Delhi; by Sultan-Sujah in Bengal; by Aurangzeb in the Deccan; by Morad-Bakche in Guzarat. Aurangzeb cajoled the latter into joining forces with him, and the two set out for Agra to take possession of the kingdom should their father be dead; "to kiss his feet should he be alive, and to deliver him from the hands of Dara." In a letter to Morad, Aurangzeb says, "I need not remind you, my brother, how repugnant to my real disposition are the toils of government. While Dara and Sultan-Sujah are tormented with a thirst for dominion, I sigh only for the life of a *fakir*."

"What, then, should Shah Jahan, this unfortunate king, do, who seeth that his sons have no regard to his orders; who is informed at all hours that they march apace towards Agra at the head of their armies, and who at this conjuncture finds himself sick, to boot, in the hands of Dara, that is, of a man who breatheth nothing but war; who prepareth for it with all the marks of an enraged resentment against his brothers? But what could he do in this extremity? He is constrained to abandon to them his treasures. He is forced to send for his old and most trusty captains, whom he knows for the most part to be not very affectionate to Dara; he must command them to fight for Dara against his own blood, his own children, and those for whom he had more esteem than for Dara; he is obliged forthwith to send armies against them all."

The first battle was a decided victory for Aurangzeb and Morad-Bakche, and they were not far from Agra.* Immediately all were in arms. An army of one hundred thousand horse, twenty thousand foot, and four thousand cannon was levied for the cause of Dara, who forced a great battle in which he was hopelessly defeated and

* In this battle the *howdah* of Prince Murad's elephant "was stuck thick with arrows as a porcupine with quills." It was long preserved as a curiosity, "also as a memorial of the bravery of a descendant of Timur."

obliged to fly in desperate case, while his victorious brothers came to the gates of Agra, where presently the emperor's guards were overpowered and he was subject to their will. "If ever man was astonished, Shah Jahan was, seeing that he was fallen into the snare which he had prepared for others, that himself was imprisoned, and Aurangzeb master of the fortress."

In a short time Morad-Bakche was imprisoned by his wily brother, and soon done to death by violence. Sultan-Sujah was defeated in a pitched battle as Dara had been, and was again. All things fell out contrary to both these vanquished and unfortunate men. By a strange accident Bernier met Dara after his worst defeat, and saw him march away with an escort of no more than five hundred cavalry, he who had led hundreds of thousands. A few days later he again saw him in chains, a prisoner, borne on an elephant through the streets of Delhi.

"This was none of those brave elephants of Ceylon or Pegu, that he was wont to ride on, with gilt harness and embroidered covers; it was an old caitiff animal, very dirty and nasty, with an old torn cover and a pitiful seat all open to the sun. There was no more seen about him that necklace of big pearls which those princes are wont to wear. All his dress was a vest of coarse linen, all dirty, with a turban of the same, and a wretched scarf over his head like a varlet."

By the vehement advice of his youngest sister, Rauchenara-Begum, he was put to death, and his bloody head was brought to Aurangzeb, that he might see; "which, when brought, he wiped it with a handkerchief, and after he was satisfied it was the very head of Dara, he fell a-weeping, saying, 'Ah, unfortunate man! Take it away and bury it.'"

The family of Dara was disposed of either by death or by imprisonment. Sultan-Sujah fled to the sea-shore by the Ganges' mouth, and after incredible sufferings perished in his flight. Shah Jahan was confined in a virtual prison until his death. The walls of his apartments were covered with gilding, but the monarch ordered them to be smeared over with rough mortar as more suited to his humbled condition; and in his last days he grew very devout.

"And thus endeth this war, which the lust of reigning had kindled among those four brothers, after it had lasted five or six years, from 1655 to 1660 or 1661, which left Aurangzeb in the peaceable possession of this puissant empire."

"To conclude, I doubt not that most of those who shall have read my history, will judge the ways taken by Aurangzeb for getting the empire very violent and horrid.

"I pretend not to plead for him, but desire only that before he be altogether condemned, reflection be made on the unhappy custom of this state, which, leaving the possession of the crown undecided, exposeth it to the conquest of the strongest. I am persuaded that those who shall a little weigh this whole history, will not take Aurangzeb for a barbarian, but for a great and rare genius, a great statesman, and a great king."

At the beginning of his reign Aurangzeb received with admirable wisdom his former tutor who had come to court expecting great advancement. The interview is reported by Bernier, directly from the recital of one who was present.

"'What is it that you would have of me? Can you reasonably desire that I should make you one of the chief noblemen of my court? Let me tell you, if you had instructed me as you should have done, nothing would have been more just. But where are those good documents you should have given me? In the first place you have taught me that all Europe was nothing but I know not what little island, of which the greatest king was he of Portugal, and next he of Holland, and after him, he of England; and as to the other kings, you have represented them to me as our petty rajahs, telling me that they tremble at the names of the kings of Indostan. Admirable geography! You should rather have taught me exactly to distinguish all those different states of the world and to well understand their strength, their way of fighting, their customs, religions, governments, and interests. I have scarce learned of you the names of my grandsires, the famous founders of this empire. You had a mind to teach me the Arabian tongue. I am much obliged to you, forsooth, for having made me lose so much time upon a language, as if the son of a king should think it to be an honor to him to be a grammarian; he to whom time is so precious for so many weighty things, which he ought betimes to learn. . . . Ought you not to have instructed me on one point, at least, so essential to be known by a king, namely, on the reciprocal duties between the sovereign and his subjects? Did you ever instruct me in the art of war, how to besiege a town, or draw up an army in battle array? Happy for me that I consulted wiser heads than thine on these subjects! Go! withdraw to thy village. Henceforth let no person know either who thou art, or what is become of thee.

"And thus did Aurangzeb resent the pedantic instructions of his tutor." *

Bernier's narrative has great merit, and it has been given consecutively without interruption from other authorities, for several reasons. In the first place, it is a recital which we can understand, since it is written by one of ourselves—an Occidental. He was especially qualified as an observer, for he was the friend and pupil of the learned Gassendi, and fully acquainted with classic and Western knowledge. He was the physician and friend of the most learned man of the court of the Great Mogul, and had special opportunities for knowing the events of the time. In one instance, at least, he is able to

* I am tempted to add in a foot-note the instructions given by the great Caliph Haroun-al-Raschid to his mentor Al-Asma'i.

"Never undertake to teach me in public, and do not be too anxious to give me advice in private. Make it your custom to wait till I ask you, and when I do so, give me a precise answer void of all superfluity. When you see that I am departing from the way of equity in my decisions, lead me back again with gentleness, and without harsh words or reprimands. Instruct me principally in such things as are most requisite for my public speeches, and never employ obscure or mysterious terms or recondite words."

There spoke a tyrant who understood human nature in general, and his own nature in particular.

report a conversation which the emperor had in private, from the direct report of his master who was present. At least one of the emperor's letters which he quotes, he actually saw in the original.

His work was written after his return to Europe, when he had no reason to tell anything but the exact truth. He had nothing to fear from the displeasure, and nothing to hope from the favor, of the court. This cannot be said for the native historians of India. They wrote for the eye and ear of the monarch, and their narratives usually represent the official view of past events. In certain cases the native author has not published his history during his lifetime, but kept it secret, and has spoken freely. His family, in this case, suffered in his stead for the posthumous publication.*

On the other hand, the native historians had the great advantage of first-hand knowledge such as a foreigner could but rarely possess.

The extracts which follow have been

* This was notably the case of Bedauni. (See Chapter IV.)

chosen from Sir Henry Elliott's invaluable collection, for the purpose of illustrating the characters of the rulers and of their times. Little attention has been paid to the historical sequence of events. Knowledge of this sort must be sought for in professed histories, like those of Elphinstone and Hunter, Mill and Elliott.

Shah Jahan.

A glimpse of Shah Jahan when he was but crown-prince is given in the narrative of Sir Thomas Roe, who says: "I never saw so settled a countenance, nor any man keep so constant a gravity, never smiling, nor in face showing any respect or difference of men, but mingled with extreme pride and contempt of all." He was then but twenty-five years old, cold, haughty, silent, a competent soldier, an able administrator. "He was flattered by some, envied by others, loved by none." The inevitable struggles for the succession to the throne of his father, Jahangir, brought him into sharp conflict with his brothers, his father, and the Empress Nur-Mahal.

The professional historian is condemned to the dreary task of following their wars and conquests if he wishes to understand the course of political events. But these events throw little light on the character of the personages. Everywhere we find the Hindu husbandman living in his village and flying at the approach of all comers. If they are on a peaceful mission, he must furnish provision for their beasts; if they are bent on war, his fields are ravaged. Above the husbandman we have the soldier, the petty chief, the over-lord, the great noble, the king—all of them warriors, and all "craving for action." Their expeditions were all alike, and the history could be prepared beforehand on one of two models—either the war was successful or not so. The same stratagems appear and reappear. On the death of a king, his sons strive for the succession. The army of each pretender, at first small, is reënforced by those who have much to gain or little to lose. The unsuccessful princes fly

THE TAJ MAHAL AT AGRA

to Persia, go on the pilgrimage to Mecca, are imprisoned for life, are blinded with hot irons, according to the degree of the discomfiture or the mildness of the king's temper. The recital of the details of these events is monotonous *à dormir debout;* unless, indeed, from time to time we can catch some glimpse of the real personality of the ruler, and hear his very accents or read his very writings.

The reign of Shah Jahan is even less eventful than that of Jahangir in these respects. It was peaceful because he left none of his rivals alive. It is memorable through the surpassing loveliness of the public buildings which he caused to be erected.

The Taj-Mahal, "a dream in marble, designed by Titans and finished by jewellers;" * the Pearl Mosque of Agra, "the

---

* Bernier says of the Taj that it was raised in honor of Taj-Bibi, Mumtaz-i-Mahal, "his wife, that extraordinary and celebrated beauty of the Indies, whom he loved so passionately that it is said he never enjoyed any other woman while she lived, and that when she died he was in danger to die himself." The Taj has been described a thousand times, but never with more delicate insight than by M. André Chevrillon in the *Revue des Deux Mondes,*

purest and loveliest house of prayer in the world;" the great mosque of Delhi; the palace of the same royal city—these noble and exquisite constructions will make his reign famous forever. The early period of cruelty to his enemies and extermination of the rival claimants to the throne was succeeded by an era of peace, prosperity, and magnificence by which alone he is now remembered.

The public buildings absorbed enormous sums. The famous "peacock throne" was alone valued at above sixty million dollars.* One of its rubies was "upwards of three fingers' breadths wide (*sic*) by two in length." This was, perhaps, the famous stone, "the tribute of the world," given by Shah Abbas of Persia to Jahangir. The royal treasuries overflowed with jewels and gold and silver.

---

vol. civ, page 91 (1891). Mumtaz-i-Mahal has no public history. While she lived the king was held captive in the tresses of her hair; she bore him many sons and daughters; at her death he was like to die; in her memory he raised the chief building of the round world: this is all her history, and it is enough.

*According to Tavernier, a French jeweller, who travelled in India.

"In the course of years many valuable gems had come into the imperial jewel-house, each one of which might serve as an eardrop for Venus." These were given to the chief goldsmith to make the famous throne. Its canopy was literally covered with gems and was supported by twelve columns set with pearls. On the top of the canopy was a peacock with extended tail thick set with gems. The three steps were incrusted with precious stones. This throne remained the wonder of India until it was carried away by Nadir-Shah, in 1739. It is still to be seen in Teheran, but its chief jewels have been displaced and dispersed. It is even now valued at thirteen million dollars.*

Tavernier the jeweller has his word to say of the Taj-Mahal. "Of all the tombs which one sees at Agra, that of the wife of Shah Jahan is the most splendid. It is at the east

* There were six other thrones, Tavernier says, and the native historians describe one which was also ornamented with peacocks, arranged two and two. See a paper by Dr. Ball, on the engraved gems of the Moguls, in *Proc. R. Irish Acad.*, vol. iii., p. 380.

end of the town, by the side of the river, in a great square surrounded by walls. This square is a kind of garden divided into compartments like our *parterres*, but in the places where we put gravel there is white and black marble. . . . I witnessed the commencement and accomplishment of this great work, on which they have expended twenty-two years, during which twenty thousand men worked incessantly. . . . Shah Jahan began to build his own tomb on the other side of the river, but the war which he had with his sons interrupted his plan, and Aurangzeb, who reigns at present, is not disposed to complete it." Tavernier has also left an expert's opinion on the crown-jewels, which he was permitted to examine at leisure. The curious in such matters should consult his *Travels in India*, edited by V. Ball.

Shah Jahan's entertainments were on a magnificent scale. The festival given on his accession, together with the presents to his officers, cost eight million dollars. His gifts to the two sacred cities were on a corresponding scale. "Among the events of this year was the despatch of a candlestick studded with gems to the revered tomb of the Prophet (in Medina), on whom be the greatest favors and blessings." The candlestick was of amber, and weighed about eighteen pounds, and it was literally covered with gems, including a monster diamond from Golconda, which alone was valued at over seventy-five thousand dollars. "One of the subject provinces was taxed to provide magnificent gifts besides, and a special embassy was sent to the holy cities under the charge of a descendant of the Prophet (on whom be the peace)." All these and other splendors were dispersed when the sacred cities were despoiled by the Wahabees.

This lavish expenditure was the mark of a peaceful and prosperous reign. The king was not oppressive, and in his later years grew to be kind; the revenue was plenty, and the surplus was devoted to immense government works. He was certainly very popular with his officers, especially in the latter part of his reign. It is to be noted that most of the anecdotes of Shah Jahan which have come down to us represent the king as always worsted in an exchange of repartee.

Rai Bhara Mal says that in Shah Jahan's happy times the prosperity of the land was greatly increased; that domains which in Akbar's reign yielded but three *lacs*, now yielded ten, and that this was the rule with some few exceptions. "Notwithstanding the great area of the country, complaints were so few that only one day in the week, Wednesday, was fixed upon for the administration of justice; and it was rarely even then that twenty plaintiffs were found."

The subordinate courts in the country districts seem to have been organized with full liberty of appeal, so that finally only cases of blood feuds and concerning religious matters came directly to the king.

Aurangzeb.

Bernier has given strong evidence to the great qualities of Aurangzeb. The native writers, each in his own way, confirm the judgment. I have extracted a few paragraphs from the very complete histories of this reign, and have given some of the emperor's own letters almost in full; but I refer to the succeeding chapter—"The Ruin of Aurangzeb"—for a masterly picture of the whole career of the puritan emperor, from his austere youth to the troubled ending of his power.

The Habits and Manners of the Emperor Aurangzeb.

"Be it known to the readers of this work that this humble slave of the Almighty is going to describe in a correct manner the excellent character, the worthy habits, and the refined morals of this most virtuous monarch, according as he has witnessed them with his own eyes."

"The emperor, a great worshipper of God by natural propensity, is remarkable for his rigid attachment to religion." He regularly makes the appointed ablutions, prayers, fasts and vigils. Several pages are devoted to a list of his meritorious acts. "In his sacred court no word of backbiting or falsehood is allowed;" which must have been a blessing in a country of intrigue, and a glaring novelty in courts.

"Under the dictates of anger or passion he never issues orders of death." "Islam is everywhere triumphant, and the Hindu temples are destroyed." "All the mosques in the empire are repaired at the public expense." A digest of all the theological works in the royal library was ordered to be prepared, so that any inquirer might satisfy himself on the points of orthodoxy. The very essence of the long reign—its *leit-motiv*—was the return from the worship of strange gods to Islam.

"The emperor himself is perfectly acquainted with the commentaries, traditions, and law; and he learned the Kuran by heart after ascending the throne. He even made two copies of it with his own hand, which he sent to the two holy cities."

"So long as nature keeps the garden of the world fresh, may the plant of the prosperity of this preserver of the garden of dignity and honor continue fruitful." The four daughters of Aurangzeb were all pious. One of them knew the Kuran by heart. Another was an Arabic and Persian scholar in prose and poetry, and learned in the Muhammadan law, having been taught under the emperor's own eyes.

It is interesting to take note of the effect of intermarriages upon the purity of blood of the (so-called) Mogul emperors. Babar was the sixth in direct descent from Tamerlane, and was of pure Turki stock in the male line. His mother, however, was a pure Mogul, a descendant of Chengiz-Khan. Babar was, therefore, partly Turki and partly Mogul. One of his wives was Maham-Begam, a relation of Sultan Husein Mirza of Herat; and Humayun, the successor of Babar, was her son. There is every reason to believe that Humayun's mother was pure Turki. Her father was a direct descendant of Tamerlane.

Humayun made a rash marriage of inclination during the period of his misfortunes and wanderings (A.D. 1541). At his brother, Prince Hindal's, camp he married the young daughter of Hindal's preceptor, Sheikh Ali Akbar Jami; she was not fourteen years of age, and far below the emperor in rank, although she was a descendant of the Prophet, and counted at least one saint among her ancestors. Her father's family was from Khorassan. Her name was Hamida.*

Akbar the Great was the son of Hamida; and his son Jahangir was born of Akbar's marriage with the daughter of a Hindu rajah, Bihari Mal.† Shah Jahan, his successor, was the son of Jahangir's first wife, the granddaughter of the Rajah Maldeo of Jodhpur.

Shah Jahan's favorite queen and the mother of all his sons was Mumtaz-i-Mahal, the niece of Nur-Mahal (Jahangir's queen), the daughter of Asaf-Khan, the granddaughter of Mirza Ghiyas Beg, a Persian. Aurangzeb, the emperor, was the son of

---

* Her *title* was Maryam Makani—dwelling with the Virgin Mary. She was not a Christian.

† Her *title* was the Maryam uzzamani—Mary of the age, of the period.

Mumtaz-i-Mahal, and had, therefore, but little Turki blood in his veins. The characters of the male ancestors are well known. Of the female we know next to nothing, excepting always the famous Empress Nur-Mahal.

In a general way the effect of the Hindu strain of blood is not difficult to trace in the characters of the successive monarchs as we follow the line from the frank, bold, generous Babar, through the humaner, and though not less adventurous, Akbar, to Jahangir, the indolent and self-indulgent king, down to Shah Jahan, who was, in his youth at least, the very model of a magnificent, cold, and aristocratic Hindu.

The chief characteristics of Aurangzeb's reign are to be attributed more to his bigoted Muhammadanism than to his temperament. When we consider that all these kings are of the stock of Chengiz-Khan and of the Amir Timur, the gradual thinning of that savage blood by the richer, more luxurious Hindu and Persian streams deserves at least this brief digression.

On occasion, Aurangzeb could be as cruel as Timur himself. When Sambha and Kabkalas were taken prisoners, and were abusive to him while in chains before the throne, he ordered their tongues to be cut out, "that they might no longer speak disrespectfully." "After that their eyes were to be torn out," and finally they, with ten others, were put to death with a variety of tortures. These were Hindus, "infidels" (not Muhammadans), however.

Shah Jahan was kept closely in the citadel at the end of his reign, and Aurangzeb communicated with him only by letters. In one of them he states his position with apparent humility, and, recounting his victories over his brothers, hopes "soon to be free of this business." "It is clear to your Majesty that Almighty Allah bestows his trusts upon one who discharges the duty of cherishing his subjects and protecting the people. It is manifest and clear to wise men that a wolf is not fit for a shepherd, and that no poor-spirited man can perform the great duty of governing. Sovereignty signifies protection of the people, not self-indulgence and libertinism." Thus proudly, though in outwardly respectful form, he justifies his course to his captive father and king, who had been a wolf and not a shepherd.

His crafty spirit appears in one of his letters to Murad Bakhsh, where he says: "I have not the slightest liking for, or wish to take any part in, the government of this deceitful and unstable world; my only desire is, that I may make the pilgrimage (to Mecca). But whatever course you may take against our brother (Dara), you may consider me your sincere friend and ally." When Murad was a prisoner in Aurangzeb's camp, it was necessary to send him away secretly, for fear of a rescue. *Four* elephants were prepared, and were sent under escort in four different directions. On one of these the captive prince was placed, but his partisans could not tell on which one, and dared not attack all four. Though Aurangzeb was endowed with every kind of courage, physical and moral, he was ever crafty and suspicious. It was not in his nature to be frankly bold like Babar; but as age came on he grew kinder and more indulgent to erring human nature, though no less distrustful of it.

> *He journeyed with Wariness, and where he halted*
> *There Wariness halted herself, his comrade.*

We have a picture of the king in the seventy-sixth year of his age, by Gemelli, a Neapolitan traveller. It is worth quotation, though it is but a superficial and trivial portrait at the best. The Neapolitan could not comprehend a nature like the emperor's.

"Soon after, the king came in, leaning on a staff forked at the top, abundance of courtiers going before him. He had on a white vest, a turban of the same white stuff, and tied with a gold web, on which an emerald of a vast bigness appeared amidst four little ones. A silk sash covered the Indian-dagger hanging at the left. His shoes were after the Moorish fashion, and his legs naked, without hose. Two servants put away the flies with long white horse-tails; another, at the same time, keeping off the sun with a green umbrella. The king was of low stature,

AURANGZEB'S MOSQUE AT BENARES

with a large nose, slender and stooping with age (he was now seventy-six years old, as has been said). The whiteness of his round beard was more visible on his olive-colored skin. When he was seated, they gave him his cimeter and buckler, which he laid down on his left side, within the throne. Then he made a sign with his hand for those that had business to draw near; who being come up, two secretaries, standing, took their petitions, which they delivered to the king, telling him their contents. I admired to see him indorse them with his own hand, without spectacles, and by his cheerful, smiling countenance seem pleased with the employment."

After the audience of the king's sons and grandsons and the great officers was over, the king retired, and the court returned to their tents, led by the provost-marshal, who was preceded by a great trumpet of green copper eight spans long. "That foolish trumpet made me laugh, because it made a noise much like that our swine-herds make to call together their swine at night."

In the fiftieth year of the reign, when he

was eighty-eight years old, Aurangzeb fell seriously ill. His son, Azam-Shah, wrote for leave to visit him, urging that the air of his station did not agree with his health. "This displeased the emperor, who replied that he had once written a letter of exactly the same effect to *his* father, Shah Jahan, when he was ill, and that he was told in answer that every air (*hawa*) was suitable to a man, except the fumes (*hawa*) of ambition."

Aurangzeb writes to his two sons not long before his death. To his heir he says: "Health to thee! My heart is near thee. Old age has arrived; weakness subdues me. I came a stranger into this world, and a stranger I depart, knowing nothing of myself, what I am, or for what I am destined. The instant which has passed in power hath left only sorrow behind it. I have not been the guardian and protector of the empire. My valuable time has been passed vainly. I have a dread for my salvation and with what torments I may be punished. Though I have strong reliance on the mercies of Allah, yet regarding my actions fear will not quit me.

Come, then, what may, I have launched my vessel in the waves. Give my last prayer to my grandson, whom I cannot see, but the desire affects me. The Begam (his daughter) appears afflicted; but Allah is the only judge of hearts. The foolish thoughts of women produce nothing but disappointment. Farewell. Farewell. Farewell."

To his younger and most beloved son, the Prince Kam-Bakhsh, he writes: "My son, nearest to my heart. . . . Now I depart a stranger, and lament my own insignificance, what does it profit me? I carry with me the fruits of my own sins and imperfections. Surprising Providence! I came here alone, and alone I depart. . . . Be cautious that none of the faithful are slain (in the troubles which he foresees will arise), or that their miseries fall upon my head. The agonies of death come fast upon me. The courtiers, however deceitful, yet must not be ill-treated. It is necessary to gain your ends by gentleness and art. I am going. . . . Whatever good or evil I have done, it was for you. . . . No one has seen the departure of his own soul, but I see that mine is departing."

To him the moral of his long reign was that all is vanity. He, like the Caliph Abdulrahman of Spain, might say: "Fifty years have I reigned, and in so long a course of time I count but fourteen days which have not been poisoned by some vexation."

When the emperor was nearly ninety years old, and had reigned fifty years, he departed to the mercy of Allah. He left a will; and in a letter he renounced the pomp of a magnificent tomb. "Carry this creature of dust quickly to the first burial place, and consign him to the earth without any useless coffin," he wrote. His funeral expenses were paid from money which he had himself earned by transcribing the Kuran, and they were limited to the smallest possible sum. According to the will of the king, his mortal remains were to be deposited in a tomb constructed during his lifetime. "A red stone three yards in length, two in width, and only a few inches in depth, is placed above the tomb. On this stone was hollowed out a place for the reception of earth and seeds, and odoriferous herbs there diffused their fragrance round about."

One of Aurangzeb's high nobles has left us an affecting account of the emperor's death. "My attachment to his majesty was so great that, observing his life to be drawing to a close, I did not wish to quit the presence. The emperor called me to him and said: 'Separation now takes place between us, and our meeting again is uncertain. Forgive, then, whatever wittingly or unwittingly I may have done against thee, and pronounce the words *I forgive*, three times, with sincerity of heart. As thou hast served me long, I also forgive thee whatever knowingly or otherwise thou mayst have done against me.' Upon hearing these words sobs became like a knot in my throat, and I had not power to speak. At last, after his majesty had repeatedly pressed me, I made a shift to pronounce the words *I forgive*, three times, interrupted by heavy sobs. He shed many tears, repeated the words, and, after blessing me, ordered me to retire."

Khafi-Khan, who knew Aurangzeb well, writes of him that "of all the sovereigns of the house of Timur, no one has ever been so distinguished for devotion, austerity, and justice. In courage, long-suffering, and sound judgment he was unrivalled. But, from reverence to the injunctions of the law, he did not make use of punishment; and without punishment the administration of a country cannot be maintained." "So every plan and project that he formed came (finally) to little good."

He was the last of the Mogul kings who can be called great.

AURANGZEB

CHAPTER VIII

THE RUIN OF AURANGZEB; OR THE HISTORY OF A REACTION *

BY SIR WILLIAM WILSON HUNTER, LL.D., K.C.S.I., C.I.E., ETC.

WHEN Dr. Johnson wanted a modern example of *The Vanity of Human Wishes,* he took the career of the Royal Swede. But during the same period that witnessed the brief glories of Charles the Twelfth in Europe, a more appalling tragedy of wrecked ambition was being enacted in the East. Within a year of Charles's birth in 1681, Aurangzeb, the last of the Great Mughals, set out with his grand army for Southern India. Within a year of Charles's fatal

* It is necessary to explicitly say in this place that the British copyright in this chapter is the property of Sir William Wilson Hunter, the author of it, by whose kind permission it is reproduced in this American book; with the authority, however, to circulate it in England and the Colonies.

EDWARD S. HOLDEN.

march to Russia in 1708, Aurangzeb's grand army lay shattered by a quarter of a century of victory and defeat; Aurangzeb himself was dying of old age and a broken heart; while his enemies feasted around his starving camp, and prayed heaven for long life to a sovereign in whose obstinacy and despair they placed their firmest hopes. The Indian emperor and the Swedish king were alike men of severe simplicity of life, of the highest personal courage, and of indomitable will. The memory of both is stained by great crimes. History can never forget that Charles broke an ambassador on the wheel, and that Aurangzeb imprisoned his father and murdered his brethren.

But here the analogy ends. As the Indian emperor fought and conquered in a wider arena, so was his character laid out on grander lines, and his catastrophe came on a mightier scale. He knew how to turn back the torrent of defeat, by commanding his elephant's legs to be chained to the ground in the thick of the battle, with a swift yet deliberate valour which Charles might have envied. He could spread the meshes of a homicidal intrigue, enjoying all the time the most lively consolations of religion; and he could pursue a State policy with humane repugnance to the necessary crimes, yet with an inflexible assent to them, which Richelieu would have admired. From the meteoric transit of Charles the Twelfth history learns little. The sturdy English satirist probably put that vainglorious career to its highest purpose when he used it 'to point a moral, or adorn a tale.' From the ruin of Aurangzeb the downfall of the Mughal Empire dates, and the history of modern India begins.

The house of Timur had brought with it to India the adventurous hardihood of the steppes, and the unsapped vitality of the Tartar tent. Babar, the founder of the Indian Mughal Empire in 1526, was the sixth in descent from Timur, and during six more generations his own dynasty proved prolific of strongly marked types. Each succeeding emperor, from father to son, was, for evil or for good, a genuine original man. In Babar himself, literally The Lion, the Mughal dynasty had produced its epic hero; in Humayun, its knight-errant and royal refugee; in Akbar, its consolidator and statesman; in Jahangir, its talented drunkard; and its magnificent palace-builder in Shah Jahan. It was now to bring forth in Aurangzeb a ruler whom hostile writers stigmatise as a cold-hearted usurper, and whom Muhammadan historians venerate as a saint.

Aurangzeb was born on the night of the 4th of November 1618, and before he reached the age of ten, his father, Shah Jahan, had succeeded to the throne of his ancestors. His mother, The Exalted of the Palace, was the last of the great queens who shared and directed the fortunes of a Mughal Emperor. Married when just out of her teens, she bore thirteen children to her husband, and died in giving birth to a fourteenth. Her nineteen years of wedded life had been splendid but sorrowful. Of her children, eight died in infancy or childhood. Her bereaved husband raised to her, in sight of his palace, the most beautiful tomb in the world. It crowns the lofty bank of the Jumna, a dream in marble, with its cupolas floating upwards like silver bubbles into the sky. To this day it bears her Persian title, The Exalted of the Palace ; a title which travellers from many far countries have contracted into the Taj Mahal.

She left behind her four sons and two daughters. Her eldest surviving child was the Princess Imperial, named the Ornament of the World ; a masterful but affectionate girl of seventeen, and not free from feminine frailties. The Princess Imperial succeeded to her mother's place in her father's heart. During the remaining twenty-seven years of his reign, she guided his policy and controlled his palace ; and during his last eight years of dethronement and eclipse, she shared his imprisonment. The great rest-house for travellers at Delhi was one of her many splendid charities. She died with the fame of her past beauty still fresh, unmarried, at the age of sixty-seven. Her grave lies close to a saint's and to a poet's, in that *campo santo* of marble latticework, and exquisite carving, and embroidered canopies of silk and gold, near the Hall of the Sixty-four Pillars, beyond the Delhi walls. But only a piece of pure white marble, with a little grass piously watered by generations, marks the princess' grave. 'Let no rich canopy surmount my resting place,' was her dying injunction, inscribed on the headstone. 'This grass is the best covering for the grave of a lowly heart, the humble and transitory Ornament of the World, the disciple of the holy Man of Chist, the daughter of the Emperor Shah Jahan.' But the magnificent mosque of Agra is the public memorial of the lady who lies in that modest grass-covered grave.

The eldest son of The Exalted of the Palace, and the heir apparent to the empire, was Prince Dara. One year younger than the Princess Imperial, he became the object of her ardent affection through life. In the troubles that were to fall upon the family she devoted herself to his cause. Dara was an open-handed, high-spirited prince, contemptuous of advice, and destitute of self-control. He had a noble and dignified bearing, except when he lost his temper. At such moments he would burst out into a tornado of abuse, insulting and menacing the greatest generals and officers of State. The rigid observances of Islam, with its perpetual round of prayers and its long fasts, were distasteful to his nature. And he had all the rival religions, Christian, Muhammadan, and Hindu to choose from, in the Court and the seraglio. Dara leaned towards Christianity and Hinduism. While contemptuously continuing in externals a Muhammadan, he concocted for himself an easy and elegant faith from the alternate teaching of a Brahman philosopher and a French Jesuit. He shocked good Mussulmans by keeping an establishment of learned Hindus to translate their infidel scriptures into Persian. He even wrote a book himself to reconcile the conflicting creeds.

His next brother Shuja was a more discreet young prince. Conciliatory to the nobles, courageous and capable of forming well-laid plans, he might also have been able to execute them, but for his love of pleasure. In the midst of critical affairs, he would suddenly shut himself up with the ladies of his palace, and give days and nights to wine, and song, and dance; no minister of State daring to disturb his revels. Like his elder brother, he too fell away from the orthodox Suni faith of the Indian Muhammadans. But Shuja's defection was due to deliberate policy. He adopted the Shia heresy of Persia, with the hope of winning the Persian adventurers, then powerful at Court and in the army, to his side in the struggle which he foresaw must take place for the throne.

Next to him in the family came the princess named The Brilliant Lady; less beautiful and less talented than her elder sister, but equally ambitious, and fonder of gifts and of display. She attached herself to the cause of the third brother Aurangzeb, born fourteen months after herself. The youngest of the four brethren was Prince Murad, six years younger than Aurangzeb. Murad grew up a model Muhammadan knight; generous, polite, a despiser of intrigue, and devoted to war and the chase. He boasted that he had no secrets, and that he looked only to his sword to win his way to fortune. But as years passed on, his shining qualities were tarnished by an increasing indulgence at the table, and the struggle for the throne found him, still a brave soldier indeed, but also a glutton and a drunkard.

In the midst of this ambitious and voluptuous Imperial family, a very different character was silently being matured. Aurangzeb, the third brother, ardently devoted himself to study. In after-life he knew the Kuran by heart, and his memory was a storehouse of the literature, sacred and profane, of Islam. He had himself a facility for verse, and wrote a prose style at once easy and dignified, running up the complete literary gamut from pleasantry to pathos. His Persian Letters to his Sons, thrown off in the camp, or on the march, or from a sick bed, have charmed Indian readers during two centuries, and still sell in the Punjab bazaars. His poetic faculty he transmitted in a richer vein to his eldest daughter, whose verses survive under her *nom de plume* of The Incognita.

But in the case of Aurangzeb, poetry and literary graces merely formed the illuminated margin of a solid and sombre learning. His tutor, a man of the old scholastic philosophy, led him deep into the ethical and grammatical subtleties which still form the too exclusive basis of an orthodox Muhammadan education. His whole nature was filled with the stern religion of Islam. Its pure adoration of one unseen God, its calm pauses for personal prayer five times each day, its crowded celebrations of public worship, and those exaltations of the soul which spring from fasting and high-strained meditation, formed the realities of existence to the youthful Aurangzeb. The outer world in which he moved, with its pageants and pleasures, was merely an irksome intrusion on his inner life. We shall presently see him wishing to turn hermit. His eldest brother scornfully nicknamed him The Saint.

To a young Muhammadan prince of this devout temper the outer world was at that time full of sadness. The heroic soldiers of the Early Empire, and their not less heroic wives, had given place to a vicious and delicate breed of grandees. The ancestors of Aurangzeb, who swooped down on India from the North, were ruddy men in boots. The courtiers among whom Aurangzeb grew up were pale persons in petticoats. Babar, the founder of the empire, had swum every river which he met with during thirty years of campaigning, including the Indus and the other great channels of the Punjab, and the mighty Ganges herself twice during a ride of 160 miles in two days. The luxurious lords around the youthful Aurangzeb wore skirts made of innumerable folds of the finest white muslin, and went to war in palankeens. On a royal march, when not on duty with the Emperor, they were carried, says an eye-witness, 'stretched as on a bed, sleeping at ease till they reached their next tent, where they are sure to find an excellent dinner,' a duplicate kitchen being sent on the night before.

A hereditary system of compromise with

strange gods had eaten the heart out of the State religion. Aurangzeb's great-grandfather Akbar, deliberately accepted that system of compromise as the basis of the empire. Akbar discerned that all previous Muhammadan rulers of India had been crushed between two opposite forces; between fresh hordes of Mussulman invaders from without, and the dense hostile masses of the Hindu population within. He conceived the design of creating a really national empire in India, by enlisting the support of the native races. He married, and he compelled his family to marry, the daughters of Hindu princes. He abolished the Infidel Tax on the Hindu population. He threw open the highest offices in the State, and the highest commands in the army, to Hindu leaders of men.

The response made to this policy of conciliation forms the most instructive episode in Indian history. One Hindu general subdued for Akbar the great provinces of Bengal and Orissa; and organised, as his finance minister, the revenue system of the

Mughal Empire. Another Hindu general governed the Punjab. A third was hurried southwards two thousand miles from his command in Kabul, to put down a Muhammadan rising in districts not far from Calcutta. A Brahman bard led an imperial division in the field, and was Akbar's dearest friend, for whose death the emperor twice went into mourning. While Hindu leaders thus commanded the armies and shaped the policy of the empire, Hindu revenue officers formed the backbone of its administration, and the Hindu military races supplied the flower of its troops. It was on this political confederation of interests, Mussulman and Hindu, that the Mughal Empire rested, so long as it endured.

Akbar had not, however, been content with a political confederation. He believed that if the empire was to last, it must be based on a religious coalition of the Indian races. He accordingly constructed a State religion, catholic enough, as he thought, to be acceptable to all his subjects. Such a scheme of a universal religion had, during two hundred years, been the dream of Hindu reformers and the text of wandering preachers throughout India. On the death of the Bengal saint of the fifteenth century, the Muhammadans and Hindus contended for his body. The saint suddenly appeared in their midst, and, commanding them to look under the shroud, vanished. This they did. But under the winding sheet they found only a heap of beautiful flowers, one-half of which the Hindus burned with holy rites, while the other half was buried with pomp by the Mussulmans. In Akbar's time, many sacred places had become common shrines for the two faiths: the Mussulmans venerating the same impression on the rocks as the footprint of their prophet, which the Hindus revered as the footprint of their god.

Akbar, the great-grandfather of Aurangzeb, utilised this tendency towards religious coalition as an instrument of political union. He promulgated a State religion, called the Divine Faith, which combined the monotheism of Islam with the symbolic worship of Hinduism, and with something of the spirit of Christianity. He worshipped the sun as the most glorious visible type of the Deity; and he commanded the people to prostrate themselves before himself as the Divine representative. The Muhammadan lawyers set their seal to a decision supporting his Majesty. The Muhammadan medical men discovered that the eating of beef, which Akbar had renounced as repugnant to Hindu sentiment, was hurtful to the human body. Poets glorified the new faith; learned men translated the Hindu scriptures and the Christian gospel; Roman priests exhibited the birth of Jesus in waxwork, and introduced the doctrine of the Trinity. The orthodox Muhammadan beard was shaved; the devout Muhammadan salutation was discontinued; the Muhammadan confession of faith disappeared from the coinage; the Muhammadan calendar gave place to the Hindu. At length, a formal declaration of apostasy was drawn up, renouncing the religion of Islam for the Divine Faith of the Emperor.

The Emperor was technically the elected

head of the Muhammadan congregation, and God's vicegerent on earth. It was as if the Pope had called upon Christendom to renounce in set terms the religion of Christ. A Persian historian declares that when these 'effective letters of damnation,' as he calls them, issued, the heavens might have rent asunder and the earth opened her abyss As a matter of fact, Akbar was a fairly successful religious founder. One or two grave men retired from his Court, and a local insurrection was easily quelled. But Akbar had no apostolic successor. His son, the talented drunkard, while he continued to exact the prostrations of the people, revived the externals of Islam at Court, and restored the Muhammadan confession of faith to the coin. Akbar's grandson, the palace-builder, abolished the prostrations. At the same time he cynically lent his countenance to the Hindu worship, took toll on its ceremonies, and paid a yearly allowance to the Hindu high priest at Benáres.

But neither the son nor the grandson of Akbar could stem the tide of immorality which rolled on, with an ever-increasing volume, during three generations of contemptuous half-belief. One of Akbar's younger sons had drunk himself to death, smuggling in his liquor in the barrel of his fowlingpiece, when his supply of wine was cut off. The quarter of Delhi known as Shaitanpara, or Devilsville, dates from Akbar's reign. The tide of immorality brought with it the lees of superstition. Witches, wizards, diviners, professors of palmistry, and miracle-workers thronged the capital. 'Here,' says a French physician at the Mughal Court, 'they tell a poor person his fortune for a halfpenny.' A Portuguese outlaw sat as wisely on his bit of carpet as the rest, practising astrology by means of an old mariner's compass and a couple of Romish prayer-books, whose pictured saints and virgins he used for the signs of the zodiac.

It was on such a world of immorality, superstition and unbelief that the austere young Aurangzeb looked out with sad eyes. His silent reflections on the prosperous apostates around him must have been a sombre monotone, perhaps with ominous passages in it, like that fierce refrain which breaks in upon the Easter evening psalm, 'But in the name of the Lord, I will destroy them.' A young prince in this mood was a rebuke to the palace, and might become a danger to the throne. No one could doubt his courage; indeed he had slain a lion set free from the intervening nets usually employed in the royal chase. At the age of seventeen, his father accordingly sent him to govern Southern India, where the Hindu Marathas and two independent Muhammadan kingdoms professing the Shia heresy, might afford ample scope for his piety and valour.

The imperial army of the south, under his auspices, took many forts, and for a time effected a settlement of the country. But after eight years of viceregal splendour, Aurangzeb, at the age of twenty-five, resolved to quit the world, and to pass the rest of his life in seclusion and prayer. His father angrily put a stop to this project; recalled him to Court, stripped him of his military rank, and deprived him of his personal estate. But next year it was found expedient to employ Aurangzeb in the government of another province; and two years later he received the great military command of Balkh. On his arrival, the enemy swarmed like locusts upon his camp. The attempt to beat them off lasted till the hour of evening prayer; when Aurangzeb calmly dismounted from his horse, kneeled down in the midst of the battle, and repeated the sacred ritual. The opposing general, awed by the religious confidence of the prince, called off his troops, saying 'that to fight with such a man is to destroy oneself.' After about seven years of wars and sieges in Afghanistan, Aurangzeb was again appointed Viceroy of Southern India.

In 1657, his eldest brother, firmly planted in the Imperial Court, and watching with impatient eyes the failing health of the Emperor, determined to disarm his brethren. He procured orders to recall his youngest brother Murad from his viceroyalty on the western coast; and to strip Aurangzeb of his power in the south. These mandates found Aurangzeb besieging one of the two heretical Muhammadan capitals of Southern India. Several of the great nobles at once deserted him. He patched up a truce with the beleaguered city, and extorted a large sum of money from its boy-king. He had previously squeezed a great treasure from the other independent Muhammadan kingdom of the south. Thus armed, at the cost of the Shia heretics, with the sinews of war, he marched north to deliver his father, the Emperor, from the evil counsels of the Prince Imperial.

For the Emperor, now sixty-seven years of age, lay stricken with a terrible disease. The poor old palace-builder well knew the two essential conditions for retaining the Mughal throne—namely, to be perfectly pitiless to his kindred, and to be in perfect health himself. In the early days of the Empire, the royal family had been knit together in bands of warm affection; and its chivalrous founder had given his own life for his son's. Bàbar, runs the story, seeing his son sinking under a mortal disease, walked three times solemnly round the bed, and implored God to take his own life and spare the prince. After a few moments of silent prayer, he suddenly exclaimed, 'I have borne it away; I have borne it away!' and from that moment his son began to recover, while the Lion Babar visibly declined. But during three generations, the Mughal dynasty had lain under the curse of bad sons. Aurangzeb's father, the stricken Emperor, had been a rebel prince. He left not one male alive of the house of Timur, so that he and his children might be the sole heirs of the Empire. These children were now to prove his perdition. Amid the pangs of his excruciating disease, his eldest son Dara grasped the central government; while the next son, Prince Shuja, hurried north from his Viceroyalty of Bengal to seize the imperial capital.

Prince Shuja was driven back. But there was a son advancing from the south whose steps could not be stayed. Aurangzeb had been forced by his eldest brother's intrigues to assume the defensive. It seems doubtful whether, at first, he aspired to the throne. His sole desire, he declared, was to rescue his father from evil counsellors, and then to retire from the world. This longing for the religious life had led to his public degradation when a young prince: it asserted itself amid the splendours of his subsequent reign. At the present crisis it served him for a mask: as to whether it was genuine, his previous and later life perhaps entitle him to the benefit of a doubt. On one point he had firmly made up his mind: that the apostasy of his two elder brothers disqualified them for a Muhammadan throne. He accordingly resolved to join his youngest brother, whose viceroyalty lay on his way north; and who, although a drunkard in private life, was orthodox in his public belief.

A five years' war of succession followed. Each one of the four brethren knew that the stake for which he played was an empire or a grave. The eldest brother, Dara, defeated by Aurangzeb and betrayed into his hands, was condemned by the doctors of the law for his apostasy to Islam, and put to death as a renegade. The second brother, Shuja, was hunted out of his viceroyalty of Bengal into the swamps of Arakan, and outraged by the barbarian king with whom he had sought shelter. The last authentic glimpse we get of him is flying across a mountain into the woods, wounded on the head with a stone, and with only one faithful woman and three followers to share his end. The destiny of the youngest brother, Murad, with whom Aurangzeb had joined his forces, for some time hung in the balance. The tenderness with which Aurangzeb, on a memorable occasion, wiped the sweat and dust from his brother's face, was probably not altogether assumed. But the more Aurangzeb saw of the private habits of the young prince, the less worthy he seemed of the throne. At last, one night, Murad awoke from a drunken sleep to find himself Aurangzeb's prisoner. His friends planned his escape; and he would have safely let himself down from the fortress, but for an alarm caused by the weeping of a lady who had shared his confinement and from whom he could not part without saying farewell. He was not allowed another chance. Aurangzeb had him tried—nominally for an old murder which he had committed when Viceroy—and executed. Having thus disposed of his three brothers, Aurangzeb got rid of their sons by slow poisoning with laudanum, and shut up his aged father in his palace till he died.

Then was let loose on India that tremendously destructive force, a puritan Muhammadan monarch. In 1658, in the same summer that witnessed the death of the puritan Protector of England, Aurangzeb, at the age of forty, seated himself on the throne of the Mughals. The narrative of his long reign of half a century is the history of a great reaction against the religious compromises of his predecessors, and against their policy of conciliation towards the native races. He set before himself three tasks: he resolved to reform the morals of the Court; to bring down the Hindus to their proper place as infidels; and to crush the two heretical Muhammadan kingdoms of southern India.

The luxurious lords soon found that they had got a very different master from the old palace-builder. Aurangzeb was an austere compound of the emperor, the soldier, and the saint; and he imposed a like austerity on all around him. Of a humble silent demeanour, with a profound resignation to God's will in the height of success as in the depths of disaster, very plainly clothed, never sitting on a raised seat in private, nor using any vessel of silver or gold, he earned his daily food by manual labour. But he doubled the royal charities, and established free eating-houses for the sick and poor. Twice each day he took his seat in court to dispense justice. On Fridays he conducted the prayers of the common people in the great mosque. During the month of fast, he spent six to nine hours a night in reading the Kuran to a select assembly of the faithful. He completed, when emperor, the task which he had begun as a boy, of learning the sacred book by heart; and he presented two copies of it to Mecca, beautifully written with his own hand. He maintained a body of learned men to compile a code of the Muhammadan law, at a cost exceeding 20,000*l.* sterling.

The players and minstrels were silenced by royal proclamation. But they were settled on grants of land, if they would turn to a better life. The courtiers suddenly became men of prayer; the ladies of the seraglio took enthusiastically to reciting the Kuran. Only the poor dancers and singers made a struggle. They carried a bier with wailing under the window of the Emperor. On his Majesty's looking out and asking the purport of the funeral procession, they answered, that "Music was dead, and that they were bearing forth her corpse." "Pray bury her deeply," replied the Emperor from the balcony, "so that henceforth she may make no more noise."

The measures taken against the Hindus seemed for a time to promise equal success. Aurangzeb at once stopped the allowance to the Hindu high-priest at Benares. Some of the most sacred Hindu temples he levelled with the ground, erecting magnificent mosques out of their materials on the same sites. He personally took part in the work of proselytism. 'His Majesty,' says a Persian biographer, 'himself teaches the holy confession to numerous infidels, and invests them with dresses of honour and other favours.' He finally restored the Muhammadan Calendar. He refused to receive offerings at the Hindu festivals, and he sacrificed a large revenue from Hindu shrines. He remitted eighty taxes on trade and religion, at a yearly loss of several millions sterling. The goods of the true believers, indeed, were for some time altogether exempted from duties; and were eventually charged only one-half the rate paid by the Hindus.

These remissions of revenue compelled Aurangzeb to resort to new taxation. When his ministers remonstrated against giving up the Hindu pilgrim-tax, he sternly declined to share the profits of idolatry, and proposed a general tax on the infidels instead. That hated impost had been abolished by Akbar in the previous century—as part of his policy of conciliation towards the Hindus. Aurangzeb revived the poll-tax on infidels, in spite of the clamours of the Hindu population. They rent the air with lamentations under the palace windows. When he went forth in state on Friday, to lead the prayers of the faithful in the great mosque, he found the streets choked with petitioners. The Emperor paused for a moment for the suppliant crowd to open; then he commanded his elephants to advance, trampling the wretched people under foot. The detested impost was unsparingly enforced. If a Hindu of rank, writes a Persian historian, met a menial of the tax-office, 'his countenance instantly changed.' So low were the native races brought, that a proclamation issued forbidding any Hindu to ride in a palankeen, or on an Arab horse, without a licence from Government.

While Aurangzeb dealt thus hardly with the Hindu population, his hand fell heavily on the Hindu princes. He vindictively remembered that the Hindu Rajputs had nearly won the throne for his eldest brother, and that their most distinguished chief had dared to remonstrate with himself. 'If your

Majesty,' wrote the brave Hindu Raja of Jodhpur, 'places any faith in books by distinction called divine, you will there be instructed that God is the God of all mankind, not the God of the Mussulmans alone. In your temples to His name, the voice of prayer is raised; in a house of images, where a bell is shaken, He is still the object of worship.' Aurangzeb did not venture to quarrel with this great military prince. He sought his friendship, and employed him in the highest and most dangerous posts. But on his death, the Emperor tried to seize his infant sons. The chivalrous blood of the Rajputs boiled over at this outrage on the widow and the orphan. They rose in rebellion; one of Aurangzeb's own sons placed himself at their head, proclaimed himself emperor, and marched against his father with 70,000 men. A bitter war of religion followed. Aurangzeb, whose cause for a time had seemed hopeless, spared not the Hindus. He burned their homesteads, cut down their fruit-trees, defiled their temples, and carried away cartloads of their gods to the capital.

There he thrust the helpless images, with their faces downwards, below the steps of the great mosque, so that they should be hourly trampled under foot by the faithful. The Rajputs, on their side, despoiled the mosques, burned the Kuran, and insulted the prayer-readers. The war ended in a sullen submission of the Hindus; but the Rajputs became thenceforth the destroyers, instead of the supporters, of the Mughal Empire.

Having thus brought low the infidel Hindus of the north, Aurangzeb turned his strength against the two heretical Muhammadan kingdoms of southern India. The conquest of the south had been the dream of the Mughal dynasty. During four generations, each emperor had laboured, with more or less constancy, at the task. To the austere conscience of Aurangzeb it seemed not only an unalterable part of the imperial policy, but an imperative religious duty. It grew into the fixed idea of his life. The best years of his young manhood, from seventeen to forty, he had spent as Viceroy of the South, against the heretic Shia kingdoms and the infidel Marathas. When the Viceroy of the South became Emperor of India, he placed a son in charge of the war. During the first twenty-three years of his reign, Aurangzeb directed the operations from his distant northern capital. But at the age of sixty-three he realised that, if he was ever to conquer the South, he must lead his armies in person. Accordingly, in 1681, he set forth, now a white-bearded man, from his capital, never to return. The remaining twenty-six years of his life he spent on the march, or in the camp, until death released him, at the age of nearly ninety, from his long labour.

Already a great sense of isolation had chilled the Emperor's heart. 'The art of reigning,' he said, 'is so delicate, that a king's jealousy should be awakened by his very shadow.' His brothers and nephews had been slain, as a necessary condition of his accession to the throne. His own sons were now impatient of his long reign. One of them had openly rebelled; the conduct of another was so doubtful that the imperial guns had to be pointed against his division during a battle. The able Persian adventurers, who had formed the most trustworthy servants of the Empire, were discountenanced by Aurangzeb as Shia heretics. The Hindus had been alienated as infidels. But one mighty force still remained at his command. Never had the troops of the Empire been more regularly paid or better equipped, although at one time better disciplined. Aurangzeb knew that the army alone stood between him and the disloyalty of his sons, between him and the hatred of the native races. He now resolved to hurl its whole weight against the two heretical Muhammadan kingdoms of southern India.

The military array of the Empire consisted of a regular army of about 400,000 men, and a provincial militia estimated as high as 4,400,000. The militia was made up of irregular levies, uncertain in number, incapable of concentration, and whose services could only be relied on for a short period. The regular army consisted partly of contingents, whose commanders received grants of territory, or magnificent allowances for their support, partly of troops paid direct from the imperial treasury. The policy of Akbar had been to recruit from three mutually hostile classes—the Suni Muhammadans of the Empire, the Shia Muhammadans from beyond the north-western frontier, and the Hindu Rajputs. The Shia generals were conspicuous for their skill, the Rajput troops for their valour. On the eve of battle the Rajput warriors bade each other a cheerful farewell for ever; not without reason, as in one of Aurangzeb's actions only six hundred Rajputs survived out of eight thousand.

The strength of the army lay in its cavalry, 200,000 strong. The pay was high, a trooper with only one horse, says Bernier, receiving not less than Rs. 25 (say 55 shillings) a month—a large sum in those days. Cavaliers with parties of four or more horses drew from 200*l.* to nearly 1,000*l.* sterling a year, while a commander of five thousand had an annual surplus of 15,000*l.* sterling, after defraying all expenses. The sons of the nobility often served as private troopers, and the path of promotion lay open to all. Originally a commander of cavalry was bound to maintain an equal number of infantry, one-fourth of them to be matchlockmen and the rest archers. But, as a matter of fact, the infantry were a despised force, consisting of 15,000 picked men around the king's person, and a rabble of 200,000 to 300,000 foot soldiers and camp-followers on the march. The matchlockmen squatted on the ground, resting their pieces on a wooden fork which they carried on their backs; 'terribly afraid,' says Bernier, 'of burning their eyelashes or long beards; and, above all, lest some *jin* or evil spirit should cause the musket to burst.' For every random shot which they fired under these disadvantages, the cavalry discharged three arrows with a good aim, at their ease. The pay of a matchlockman went as high as 44*s.* a month.

The artillery consisted of a siege-train, throwing balls up to 96 and 112 pounds; a strong force of field-guns; 200 to 300 swivel guns on camels; and ornamental batteries of light guns, known as the stirrup-artillery. The stirrup-artillery on a royal march numbered 50 or 60 small brass pieces, mounted on painted carriages, each drawn by two horses, with a third horse led by an assistant driver as a relay. At one time many of the gunners had been Christians or Portuguese, drawing 22*l.* sterling *per mensem.* The monthly pay of a native artilleryman under Aurangzeb was about 70*s.* The importance of the artillery may be estimated from the fact, that after a battle with one of his brothers, Aurangzeb found 114 cannon left on the field. The army of Kandahar in 1651 carried with it 30,000 cannon-balls, 400,000 lbs. of gun-powder, and 14,000 rockets. The war elephants were even more important than the artillery. Experienced generals reckoned one good elephant equal to a regiment of 500 cavalry; or, if properly supported by matchlockmen, at double that number. Elephants cost from 10,000*l.* downwards: 500*l.* to 1,000*l.* being a common price. Akbar kept 5,000 of these huge animals, 'in strength like a mountain, in courage and ferocity lions.' Under Aurangzeb, over 800 elephants were maintained in the royal stables, besides the large number employed on service and in the provinces.

A pitched battle commenced with a mutual cannonade. The guns were placed in front, sometimes linked together with chains of iron. Behind them were ranged the camel-artillery with swivel-guns, supported by the matchlockmen; the elephants were kept as much as possible out of the first fire; the cavalry poured in their arrows from either flank. The Emperor, on a lofty armour-plated elephant, towered conspicuous in the centre; princes of the blood or powerful chiefs commanded the right and left wings. But there was no proper staff to enable the Emperor to keep touch with the wings and the rear. After the cannonade had done its work of confusion, a tremendous cavalry charge took place; the horse and elephants being pushed on in front and from either flank to break the adverse line of guns. In the hand-to-hand onset that followed, the centre division and each wing fought on its own account; and the commander-in-chief might consider himself fortunate if one of his wings did not go over to the enemy. If the Emperor descended from his elephant, even to pursue the beaten foe on horseback, his own troops might in a moment break away in panic, and the just won victory be turned into a defeat.

With all its disadvantages, the weight of this array was such that no power then in India could, in the long run, withstand. Its weak point was not its order of battle, but the disorder of its march. There was no complete chain of subordination between the divisional commanders. A locust multitude of followers ate up the country for leagues on either side. The camp formed an immense city sometimes five miles in length, sometimes seven and a half miles in circumference. Dead beasts of burden poisoned the air. 'I could never,' writes Bernier, in words which his countryman Dupleix turned into action a century later, 'see these soldiers, destitute of order, and moving with the irregularity of a herd of animals, without thinking how easily five and twenty thousand of our veterans from Flanders, under Condé or Turenne, would destroy an Indian army, however vast.'

A Bundela officer in the grand army has left a journal of its operations, but without mentioning the total number of troops employed. Aurangzeb found two distinct powers in southern India : first, the heretical Muhammadan kingdoms of Golconda and Bijapur ; second, the fighting Hindu peasantry, known as the Marathas. In the previous century, while Akbar was conciliating the Hindu Rajputs of the north, the independent Muhammadan sovereigns of the south had tried a like policy toward the Hindu Marathas, with less success. During a hundred years, the Marathas had sometimes sided with the independent Muhammadan kingdoms against the imperial troops, sometimes with the imperial troops against the independent Muhammadan kingdoms ; exacting payment from both sides ; and gradually erecting themselves into a third party which held the balance of power in the south. After several years of fighting, Aurangzeb subdued the two Muhammadan kingdoms, and set himself to finally crush the Hindu Marathas. In 1690 their leader was captured; but he scornfully rejected the Emperor's offer of pardon coupled with the condition of turning Mussalman. His eyes were burned in their sockets with a red-hot iron, and the tongue which had blasphemed the Prophet was cut out. The skin of his head, stuffed with straw, was insultingly exposed throughout the cities of southern India.

These and similar atrocities nerved with an inextinguishable hatred the whole Maratha race. The guerilla war of extermination which followed during the next seventeen years has scarcely a parallel in history. The Marathas first decoyed, then baffled, and finally slaughtered the imperial troops. The chivalrous Rajputs of the north had stood up against the shock of the grand army and had been broken by it. The Hindu peasant confederacy of the south employed a very different strategy. They had no idea of bidding farewell to each other on the eve of a battle, or of dying next day on a pitched field. They declined altogether to fight unless they were sure to win; and their word for victory meant 'to plunder the enemy.' Their clouds of horsemen, scantily clad, with only a folded blanket for a saddle, rode jeeringly round the imperial cavalry swathed in sword-proof wadding, or fainting under chain-armour, and with difficulty spurring their heavily caparisoned steeds out of a prancing amble. If the imperial cavalry charged in force, they charged into thin air. If they pursued in detachments, they were speared man by man.

In the Mughal army the foot-soldier was an object of contempt. The Maratha infantry were among the finest light troops in the world. Skilled marksmen, and so agile as almost always to be able to choose their own ground, they laughed at the heavy cavalry of the Empire. The Marathas camped at pleasure around the grand army, cutting off supplies, dashing in upon its line of march, plundering the ammunition-waggons at river-crossings, and allowing the wearied imperialists no sleep by night-attacks. If they did not pillage enough food from the royal convoys, every homestead was ready to furnish the millet and onions which was all they required. When encumbered with booty, or fatigued with fighting, they vanished into their hill forts; and next morning fresh swarms hung upon the imperial line of march. The tropical heats and rains added to the miseries of the northern troops. One autumn a river overflowed the royal camp at midnight, sweeping away ten thousand men, with countless tents, horses, and bullocks. The destruction only ceased when the aged Emperor wrote a prayer on paper with his own hand, and cast it into the rising waters.

During ten years Aurangzeb directed these disastrous operations, chiefly from a headquarters' cantonment. But his headquarters had grown into an enormous assemblage, estimated by an Italian traveller at over a million persons. The Marathas were now plundering the imperial provinces to the north, and had blocked the line of communication with upper India. In 1698 the Emperor, lean, and stooping under the burden of eighty years, broke up his headquarters, and divided the remnants of his forces into two *corps d'armée.* One of them he sent under his best general to hold the Marathas in check in the open country. The other he led in person to besiege their cities and hill forts. The *corps d'armée* of the plains was beguiled into a fruitless chase from province to province ; fighting nineteen battles in six months. It marched and counter-marched, writes the Bundela officer, 3,000 miles in one continuous campaign, until the elephants, horses, and camels were utterly worn out.

The Emperor's *corps d'armée* fared even worse. Forty years before, in the struggle for the throne, he had shared the bread of the common soldiers, slept on the bare ground, or reconnoitred, almost unattended, several leagues in front. The youthful spirit flamed up afresh in the aged monarch.

He marched his troops in the height of the rainy season. Many of the nobles, having lost their horses, had to trudge through the mire on foot. Fort after fort fell before his despairing onslaught; but each capture left his army more shattered and the forces of the enemy unimpaired. At last his so-called sieges dwindled into an attack on a fortified village of banditti, during which he was hemmed in within his own entrenchments. In 1703 the Marathas had surprised an imperial division on the banks of the Narbada, 21,000 strong, and massacred or driven it pell-mell into the river, before the troopers could even saddle their horses. In 1705 the imperial elephants were carried off from their pasture-ground outside the royal camp; the convoys from the north were intercepted; and grain rose to fivepence a pound in the army—a rate more than ten times the ordinary price, and scarcely reached even in the severest Indian famines when millions have died of starvation. The Marathas had before this begun to recover their forts. The Emperor collected the wreck of his army, and tried to negotiate a truce. But the insolent exultation of the enemy left him no hope. 'They plundered at pleasure,' says the Bundela officer, 'every province of the south;' 'not a single person durst venture out of the camp.'

In 1706, a quarter of a century since the grand army had set forth from the northern capital, the Emperor began to sink under the accumulation of disasters. While he was shut up within his camp in the far south, the Marathas had organised a regular system of extorting one-fourth of the imperial revenue from several of the provinces to the north. In the northwest the Hindu Rajputs were in arms. Still further north, the warlike Jat Hindu peasantry were up in revolt, near the capital. Aurangzeb had no one to quell this general rising of the Hindu races. The Muhammadan generals, who had served him so well during his prime of life, now perceived that the end was near, and began to shift for themselves. Of his four surviving sons, he had imprisoned the eldest during six years; and finally released him only after eleven years of restraint. The next and most favoured son so little trusted his father that, after one narrow escape, he never received a letter from the Emperor without turning pale. The third son had been during eighteen years a fugitive in Persia from his father's vengeance, wearying the Shah for an army with which to invade Hindustan. The fourth son had known what it was to be arrested on suspicion. The finances had sunk into such confusion that the Emperor did not dare to discuss them with his ministers. With one last effort, he retreated to Ahmadnagar; the Marathas insulting the line of march, but standing aside to allow the litter of the Emperor to pass, in an awed silence.

The only escape left to the worn-out Emperor was to die. 'I came a stranger into the world,' he wrote to one of his sons a few days before the end, 'and a stranger I depart. I brought nothing with me, and, save my human infirmities, I carry nothing away. I have fears for my salvation, and of what torments may await me. Although I trust in God's mercy, yet terror will not quit me. But, come what may, I have launched my barque on the waves. Farewell, farewell, farewell!' The fingers of the dying monarch kept mechanically telling his beads till the last moment. He expired on the 21st of February, 1707, in the 91st year of his age and the 51st of his reign according to the Muhammadan calendar; or two years less by our reckoning of time. 'Carry this creature of dust to the nearest burying-place,' he said, 'and lay it in the earth without any useless coffin.' His will restricted his funeral expenses to ten shillings, which he saved from the sale of work done with his own hands. Ninety odd pounds that he had earned by copying the Kuran, he left to the poor. His followers buried him beside the tomb of a famous saint, near the deserted capital of Daulatabad.

Never since the Assyrian summer night when the Roman Emperor Julian lay dying of the javelin wound in his side, had an imperial policy of reaction ended in so complete a catastrophe. The Roman Empire was destined to centuries of further suffering before it passed through death into new forms of life. The history of Aurangzeb's successors is a swifter record of ruin. The Hindu military races closed in upon the Mughal Empire; its Muhammadan viceroys carved out for themselves independent kingdoms from its dismembered provinces. A series of puppet monarchs were set up and pulled down; seven devastating hosts poured into India through the northern passes; a new set of invaders who would take no denial landed from the sea. Less than a century after Aurangzeb's death, Lord Lake, on his entry into Delhi, was shown a feeble old captive of the Hindu Marathas, blinded, poverty-stricken, and half imbecile, sitting under a tattered canopy, whom he compassionately saluted as the Mughal Emperor. A new rule succeeded in India; a rule under which the too rapid reforms of Akbar, and the too obstinate reaction of Aurangzeb, are alike impossible.

Periods of progress have alternated with periods of pause. But the advance has been steady towards that consciousness of solidarity, that enlightenment of the masses and that capacity for political rights, which mark the growth of a nation. It was by the alienation of the native races that the Mughal Empire perished; it is by the incorporation of those races into a loyal and united people that the British rule will endure.

> *And ye, that read these Ruines Tragicall,*
> *Learne, by their losse, to love the low degree;*
> *And, if that Fortune chaunce you up to call*
> *To Honour's seat, forget not what you be:*
> *For he, that of himself is most secure,*
> *Shall finde his state most fickle and unsure.*

THE CONQUESTS OF INDIA—APPENDIX

ALEXANDER THE GREAT entered India 327 B.C., and with his invasion our accurate knowledge of the country begins. The empire of Chandra-Gupta was formed on the remains of Alexander's conquest, and endured from 316 to 292 B.C. His grandson, the mild and pious Asoka (264–223 B.C.), established Buddhism throughout all India, even to Ceylon. An Indian embassy was sent to Cæsar Augustus in Rome (22–20 B.C.), and many coins of the reigns of Nero and Tiberius have been found buried in India in recent times. Buddhism was superseded in India at about the period when Muhammadanism was rising in Arabia. Muhammad died in 632 A.D., and thirty-two years later India was invaded by his followers; and again in 711 and 977. The great Mahmud (977 to 1010) conquered the country from

Persia to the Ganges, and established an empire which lasted till 1186, when it was overthrown by the Afghans of Ghor. Muhammad Ghori was assassinated in 1206, and one of his slaves, a viceroy, founded a dynasty, with its capital at Delhi, which existed till 1288.

The third great conqueror was Allah-ud-din-Khilji (1294–1316), whose successful generals (specially Malik Kafur) overran even the remotest regions of Southern India. A successful revolt (1321) founded the Tughlak dynasty, which endured till about 1400 A.D. Muhammad Tughlak, the second of the house, removed his capital from Delhi to the Deccan. Gradually his subordinate kings threw off their allegiance and set up independent states. The Afghan kingdoms of Bengal date from about 1336. This dismemberment of the country favored the progress of the fourth great invader, Timur.

Timur's invasion was in 1398. After fearful victories and slaughters, he returned to Samarkand, which was the central city of the many petty kingdoms parcelled out to his descendants.

India was left in confusion, ruled by Hindu, by Afghan, by Turki kings and rajahs, and all at war. Babar, the sixth in descent from Timur, invaded India in 1525, and founded the Mogul Empire, so called, which lasted, theoretically at least, till the mutiny of 1857. Its real unity and power ended with the reign of Aurangzeb in 1707.

Babar's was the first conquest of India; all the previous invasions had been mere *razzias* in search of plunder. His son Humayun simply succeeded in not losing the empire; his grandson Akbar organized and consolidated the Mogul power. The son and grandson of Akbar (Jahangir and Shah Jahan) ruled over a magnificent and fairly homogeneous realm. With Aurangzeb's long reign the solidarity of the empire ended forever.

The principal dates in the period referred to in this book are collected in what follows, for convenience. In most cases they are simply copied from Sir W. W. Hunter's admirable book, *The Indian Empire: Its People, History, and Products* (Trübner's Oriental Series).

	A.D.
Irruption of the Moguls under Timur (Tamerlane)	1398–99
Timur captures Delhi	1398
Babar—sixth in descent from Timur—born	1483
" becomes king of Ferghana	1494
" conquers Samarkand	1497
" conquers Kabul	1504
" invades India	1526
" dies	1530
Humayun—Babar's son—succeeds	1530
" capture of Lahore and occupation of the Punjab by his brother Kamran	1530
" campaigns in Malwa and Guzarat	1532
" defeated by Sher-Shah, the Afghan ruler of Bengal; retreat to Agra	1539
" finally defeated by Sher-Shah; escapes to Persia as an exile; Sher-Shah ascends the Delhi throne	1540
" returns to India; defeat of the Afghans by his young son Akbar; dies, and is succeeded by Akbar	1556
Akbar—son of Humayun—born at Amarkat in Sind	1542
" succeeds to the throne under the regency of Bairam Khan	1556

	A.D.
Akbar—assumes direct management of the kingdom; quells revolt of Bairam Khan...	1560
" invasion of the Panjab by Akbar's rival brother Hakim, who is defeated......	1566
" subjugates the Rajput kingdoms to the Mogul Empire..................	1561–68
" campaign in Guzerat, and its annexation to the empire....................	1572–73
" reconquest of Bengal, which is finally annexed to the empire.................	1576
" insurrection in Guzerat (1581–93) which is finally subjugated to the empire....	1593
" conquest of Kashmir..................	1586
" conquest of Sind......................	1592
" subjugation of Kandahar, and consolidation of the Mogul Empire over all India north of the Vindhya mountains, as far as Kabul and Kandahar.............	1594
" unsuccessful campaign of Akbar's son, Prince Murad, in the Deccan.........	1595
" Akbar's campaign in the Deccan	1599
" annexation of Khandesh, and return of Akbar to Northern India............	1601
" dies at Agra..........................	1605
Jahangir—succeeds his father Akbar	1605
" flight, rebellion, and imprisonment of his eldest son Khusru..............	1606
" marries *Nur-Mahal*................	1611
" Sir Thomas Roe's embassy arrives at his court..........................	1615

	A.D.
Jahangir—Kandahar captured by the Persians....	1621
" Rebellion of Shah Jahan, his son...	1623–25
" Mahabet-Khan seizes the emperor....	1626
" recovers his liberty; Mahabet-Khan and Shah Jahan in rebellion........	1627
" dies..............................	1627
Shah Jahan—*Nur-Mahal* imprisoned............	1627
" ascends the throne..................	1628
" Afghan uprisings in Northern India..........................	1628–30
" death of his wife *Mumtaz-i-Mahal*..	1630
" wars in the Deccan	1629–35
" Kandahar reconquered by the Moguls	1637
" temporary invasion of Balkh by the Moguls........................	1645
" *Nur-Mahal* dies.....................	1645
" Balkh abandoned by the Moguls....	1647
" Kandahar finally taken and held by the Persians.....................	1653
" war in the Deccan under Aurangzeb	1655–56
" disputes as to the succession to the throne between the four sons of Shah Jahan....................	1657–58
" dies..............................	1666
Aurangzeb—deposes Shah Jahan, his father......	1658
" Dara, his brother, executed.........	1659
" Shuja, his brother, flies and perishes miserably.........................	1660

	A.D.
Aurangzeb—Murad, his brother, imprisoned and executed	1661
" Maratha wars, under Sivaji, who rebels	1662–65
" war in the Deccan ; defeat of the Moguls	1666
" Sivaji makes peace, and obtains favorable terms	1667
" Sivaji ravages the Deccan	1670
" Sivaji defeats the Mogul army	1672
" the emperor revives the poll-tax on non-Muhammadans	1667
" war with the Rajputs	1679
" Maratha successes in the Deccan	1672–80
" the emperor in person invades the Deccan	1683
" guerrilla wars with the Marathas	1692
" the Maratha wars ; successes of the Moguls	1699–1701
" the Marathas successful	1702–05
" retreats	1706
" and dies	1707

A GENEALOGICAL TABLE OF THE HOUSE OF TIMUR

[ABRIDGED FROM PROFESSOR BLOCHMANN'S AIN-I-AKBARI.]

I. TIMUR, *b.* A.H. 736 (A.D. 1336); *d.* A.H. 807 (A.D. 1405); *buried* at Samarkand.

II. JALALUDDIN MIRAN SHAH (third son of I.), *b.* A.H. 769; *d.* A.H. 810.

III. SULTAN MUHAMMAD MIRZA (sixth son of II.), *b.* ? ; *d.* ?

IV. SULTAN ABUSAID MIRZA (eldest son of III.), A.H. 830; *d.* A.H. 873.

V. OMAR-SHAIKH MIRZA (fourth son of IV.), *b.* A.H. 860; *d.* A.H. 899 (A.D. 1494).

VI. BABAR (eldest son of V.), *b.* A.H. 888 (A.D. 1483); *d.* A.H. 937 (A.D. 1530); *buried* at Kabul. Babar had two brothers, viz.: 2. JAHANGIR MIRZA. 3. NAZIR MIRZA.

VII. HUMAYUN (eldest son of VI.), *b.* A.H. 913 (A.D. 1508); *d.* A.H. 963 (A.D. 1556); *buried* at Delhi. HUMAYUN had three brothers, viz.: 2. KAMRAM MIRZA. 3. ASKARI MIRZA. 4. MIRZA HINDAL.

VIII. AKBAR (eldest son of VII.), *b.* A.H. 949 (A.D. 1542); *d.* A.H. 1014 (A.D. 1605); *buried* at Agra.

AKBAR had two brothers, viz.: 2. MIRZA MUHAMMAD HAKIM, King of Kabul. 3. SULTAN IBRAHIM.

IX. JAHANGIR (third son of VIII.), *b.* A.H. 977 (A.D. 1569); *d.* A.H. 1037 (A.D. 1627); *buried* at Lahore. JÁHANGIR had four brothers, viz.: 1, 2. HASAN and HUSAIN (twins, died in infancy). 4. SULTAN MURAD. 5. SULTAN DANYAL.

X. SHAH JAHAN (third son of IX.), *b.* A.H. 1000 (A.D. 1591); *d.* A.H. 1076 (A.D. 1666); *buried* at Agra. SHAH JAHAN had four brothers, viz.: 1. SULTAN KHUSRU. 2. SULTAN PARWIZ. 4. JAHANDAR. 5. SHAHRYAR.

XI. AURANGZEB (third son of X.), *b.* A.H. 1027 (A.D. 1618); *d.* A.H. 1118 (A.D. 1707); *buried* at Daulatabad. AURANGZÉB had eight brothers, of whom we need only mention: 1. DARA SHIKOH. 2. SULTAN SHUJÁ. 6. MURAD BAKHSH.

Finis